CONTOURS OF GREAT LEADERSHIP

The Science, Art, and Wisdom of Outstanding Practice

Rosemary Papa, Fenwick English, Frank Davidson, Mary K. Culver, and Ric Brown

ROWMAN & LITTLEFIELD EDUCATION

A division of
ROWMAN & LITTLEFIELD PUBLISHERS, INC.
Lanham • New York • Toronto • Plymouth, UK

Published by Rowman & Littlefield Education
A division of Rowman & Littlefield Publishers, Inc.
A wholly owned subsidiary of
The Rowman & Littlefield Publishing Group, Inc.
4501 Forbes Boulevard, Suite 200, Lanham, Maryland 20706
www.rowman.com

10 Thornbury Road, Plymouth PL6 7PP, United Kingdom

British Library Cataloguing in Publication Information Available

Library of Congress Cataloging-in-Publication Data

Contours of great leadership : the science, art, and wisdom of outstanding
practice / Rosemary Papa . . . [et al.].
    p. cm.
  Includes bibliographical references and index.
  ISBN 978-1-61048-830-3 (cloth : alk. paper) — ISBN 978-1-61048-831-0
(pbk. : alk. paper) — ISBN 978-1-61048-832-7 (electronic)
  1. Educational leadership. 2. School management and organization. 3. School
administrators. I. Papa, Rosemary.
  LB2806.C58 2013
  371.2—dc23

2012041553

Printed in the United States of America.

DEDICATION

On behalf of all school district leaders
who ensure the democratic ideals of public education for all students,
for districts we have recently visited:
Calvin Baker, Vail USD
Frank Davidson, Casa Grande USD
Cindy Didway, Crane Elementary School District, Yuma
Jennifer Johnson, Glendale Union High School District
for superintendents who assisted:
Vicki Balentine, Amphitheatre Public Schools
Debbi C. Burdick, Superintendent, Cave Creek Unified Schools
Cecilia E. Johnson, Superintendent, Coolidge Unified School District
Gail Malay, Superintendent,
Lake Havasu Unified School District No. 1
Lynn Thompson, Assistant Superintendent, Crane Schools
Douglas P. Watson, Superintendent,
Winslow Unified School District #1
and for just such students,
Josephine Rosemary
Margaret Cheri
Dominic
Nolan David

CONTENTS

Figures and Tables   ix

Preface   xi

Foreword by Dick Flanary   xv

1 A Prism for Understanding Great Leadership   1
   The Nature of Educational Leadership   2
   A Model to Discuss Educational Leadership   4
   The Fluid Nature of Identity   6
   The Nature of *Accoutrements*   9
      The Critical Questions in School Culture   11
      Bourdieu's Concept of Reflexivity vs. Reflective Thinking   12
      More Than "Reflective Evaluation Craft"   13
      An Example of Reflexivity: Rational Choice Theory
         as a Silent Presupposition   15
   Chapter Learning Extensions   17
      Testing Your Understanding of This Chapter about Great Leaders   17

2 Habits of Reflection and Focus on Instruction   19
   Maturation of Leadership   20
   Shared Leadership   21
   Focus on Instruction   22

Hands-On Instructional Leadership   24
Optimism   27
Working Together   28
Habitual Values Reflection   30
Chapter Learning Extensions   32
   Testing Your Understanding of This Chapter about Values   32

3 The Most Important Knowledge Begins with Self   33
The Second Kind of Knowledge: The Anchor of
   Professional Practice   34
Professional Practice Based on Dogma Leads to Tragic Mistakes 35
The Fallacy of "Research-Based" Knowledge as Superior   37
Ipsa Scientia Potestas Est: The Politics of Knowledge   38
   1. Current Issue Analysis: The Great Leaders
     Mentoring Knowledge   39
   2. Current Issue Analysis: Leading Curriculum Improvement   40
   3. Current Issue Analysis: Student Retention in Theory and
     in Practice   41
   4. Current Issue Analysis: Technology and Its Role in Teaching
     and Learning/Social Media   42
   5. Current Issue Analysis: Trends of the Day in Common
     Core State Standards   44
   6. Current Issue Analysis: Families and Communities   46
Chapter Learning Extensions   46
   Testing Your Understanding of This Chapter about Knowledge   46

4 The Acquisition and Refinement of Skills and Insights
to Inspire Others   49
Great Leaders Prioritize Teaching and Learning   53
Great Leaders Build Strong Connections   56
Great Leaders Maintain a Disciplined Focus   58
Great Leaders Learn to Manage Efficiently *in Order*
   to Lead Effectively   60
Great Leaders Choose to Be Optimists   63
Chapter Learning Extensions   65
   Testing Your Understanding of This Chapter about Skills   65

5 Leadership Identity, Practice, and Wisdom   67
An Historic Example of an *Accoutrement* for All Time: Jeanne d'Arc   68
The American Jeanne d'Arc: Rosa Parks   69

From an Angry Young Man to a Person of *Ubuntu*: An Example
 of Self-Transformation 70
The Multifaceted Nature of Human Identity 71
Contextual Changes: How the Model of *Accoutrements* Works 73
Contextual Challenges to Educational Leadership 75
Learning How to Become Great Leaders 79
Chapter Learning Extensions 81
 Testing Your Understanding of This Chapter about Identity 81

6 The Continuing Quest to Discern Leadership Contours 83
Chronology of the Line of Inquiry 84
 Best Practices in High-Performing Elementary Schools 85
 Best Practices in High-Performing Middle/Junior and High Schools 85
The Future Demographics of America: Microcosm Arizona 86
 Arizona Superintendents 87
 Principals-in-Training 88
 Arizona High Achieving Schools Administrator Focus Groups 88
The Quest of Identity through the Contours of Leadership 89
 1. Leading Adult Learners 90
 2. Developing Compassion as Human Agency 90
 3. Acknowledging Ignored but Intended Skills 90
 4. Encouraging Intellectual Curiosity 90
 5. Understanding Futurity 91
 6. Exploring Imaginativeness 91
Chapter Learning Extensions 93
 Testing Your Understanding of This Chapter about Contours 93

Appendix A: Learning Extensions Authors' Commentary 95

Appendix B: A Brief Description of the Contexts of Great Leadership 101

Appendix C: A Chronology of Peer-Reviewed Research
 on the *Accoutrements* 105

References 109

Index 121

About the Authors 125

FIGURES AND TABLES

FIGURES

1.1 Educational Leadership as Performance in Context   5

1.2 Poor to Great Educational Leadership   7

1.3 Bourdieu's Concept of Reflexivity vs. Reflective Thinking   15

5.1 Context, Culture, Reflect   74

TABLES

1.1 The Critical Dimensions of School Culture   12

1.2 What Do You Believe about Great Leaders?   18

2.1 What Do You Believe about Values?   32

3.1 What Do You Believe about Knowledge?   47

4.1 What Do You Believe about Skills?   66

5.1   The Statistically Significant Intersection of Gender, Age,
and Education and Factors Associated with the Wheeler
2012 Study of Superintendent Turnover in North Carolina   76

5.2   The Statistically Significant Interaction between Specific Factors
and Challenges Confronting Superintendents Which Lead to
Superintendent Turnover in the Wheeler 2012 Study   78

5.3   The Movement from the Principalship to the Superintendency:
An Example of Leadership *Accoutrement*   80

5.4   What Do You Believe about Identity?   82

6.1   What Do You Believe about Contours?   94

PREFACE

Contours of Great Leadership represents a deliberate effort to plow a new furrow in the landscape of leadership books. Individually the earmarks of the book are not entirely new, but we think applied collectively they create an expanded and improved view of what constitutes great leadership in education. Here are the dimensions the authors believe represent that perspective:

A HOLISTIC VIEW OF LEADERSHIP PRACTICE: MORE THAN A BSF LOCUS

The perspective in this book is that leadership practice is not only a science, but an art form. The traditions of study in educational leadership are heavily anchored in the behavioral sciences. Most students are introduced to the field from a highly rationalistic, behavioral/structural/functional locus (BSF). And while this approach reveals some interesting dimensions of leadership, it also blurs and erases many others.

For example, the behavioral/structural/functional view is largely insensitive to the moral issues of leadership, placing its central focus on matters of efficiency and rational indices of measurable effectiveness. In education this approach has resulted in a set of national standards that only partially describe what we have chosen to call "great" educational leadership. While skills are important to be an effective leader, a "great" educational leader has to have much, much more.

To this extent the idea of *greatness* subsumes *effective*. The authors acknowledge that *greatness* is more than skills or values. *Greatness* is the totality of a leader's being, that leader's insights and intuition or "horse sense" when faced with a crisis or situations that are unique. These are the ineluctable qualities not easily measured or even objectively assessed. They amount to the ability of humans to take into account certain human qualities that are felt, such as intuition, and which translate into credibility or even charisma.

We don't believe, nor does the evidence we have examined merit the view, that the essential leadership qualities for greatness are genetic or even "traits." There are so many examples of human beings who ended up as leaders and seemed to lack these qualities when their leadership journey began to negate that perspective. We posit that such "qualities" are acquired and that they were acquired in the process of learning to lead.

We also believe that formal leadership study is an essential building block of the acquisition of not only the skills and values, but of the possible conceptual maps that may be later employed by educational leaders. We think that context is everything, and therefore preparation in educational leadership acquired within schools and school systems is essential.

LEADERSHIP AS AN ACT OF *ACCOUTERING*

To this act of acquiring learning to lead we have given the name *accoutering* following the continuing research of Rosemary Papa over her long career in the field. *Accoutering* is a deliberate act of bringing together all of the experiences, knowledges, skills, and values that result for some in becoming "great" leaders. And we see the mantle of greatness not as any permanent state that once attained lasts forever. Rather it is earned and re-earned in context after context. As it can be gained, it can also be lost. We see it as context codependent. In that respect the context makes for greatness as well as the response within the context.

Great leaders face great obstacles. The idea of sewing together a garment as an apt metaphor for learning to lead is also a contribution of a largely feminine view of leadership practice. It is a patient and persistent process of weaving together context, character, and competence over an extended period of time.

REFLEXIVE VS. REFLECTIVE PRACTICE

There are a lot of texts in the leadership field about the necessity of *reflective practice*. While there are many definitions, we believe they can be summed up as a method to think about what actions attain what results and how such actions from a leader will lead to improved results, however defined. We have adopted Pierre Bourdieu's *reflexive practice* as an additional step for "great" educational leadership.

Reflexive practice is not concerned so much about results or outcomes, but rather an examination of how a leader is thinking about his or own thinking. Another way to explain it is that *reflective practice* is thinking about thinking inside out. *Reflexive practice* is thinking about thinking outside in.

To provide an example, the ISLLC/ELCC standards largely identify skills, knowledges, and values within one type of approach to educational problem solving. The *reflective leadership practitioner* would accept such lists of skills, knowledges, and values as inclusive and work to acquire and perfect them. The *reflexive leadership practitioner* would question the nature of the standards themselves. That leader would seek to understand what skills, knowledges, and attitudes were omitted from the standards and the reasons for their omission. It would also seek to examine all of the assumptions upon which those standards rest.

Such a leader would be asking the question, "Who benefits from the acquisition and application of these standards, and who doesn't?" Such a question would reveal the vested interests at play. We believe that *leadership* as *accoutering* involves both reflective and reflexive practice.

The authors of the book have incorporated the idea of both *reflective* and *reflexive* thinking into the *learning extensions* at the end of each chapter. These extensions serve as a heuristic device to enable the reader to determine his/her own knowledge about the concepts discussed in each chapter and then to think about them in alternative ways.

LEADERSHIP IS A CONSTANT PROCESS OF BECOMING

All of the authors of this book have been practitioners, and at least one remains an incumbent school superintendent. We are not armchair theorists but have lived the consequences of the decisions we have made as educational leaders. Leadership is a constant process of becoming. We have suffered our share of successes and defeats. We have learned from both. A leader's work is never done. There is always more to do and more to learn.

Great leadership involves human learning until we cease to exist. Even with death great leaders continue to influence us by providing the basis for inspiration, dedication, wisdom, persistence, and hope. The truth of the matter is that great leaders remain the wellsprings of human endeavor into time. As their legacy grows they attain a kind of continuing immortality in our lives and those that follow us.

We respectfully dedicate our book to those leaders who continue to provide exemplars for living, loving, and leading in the education profession.

FOREWORD

Contours of Great Leadership is a must read for all educators interested in a thorough, compelling, and unique view of leadership. Leadership matters in schools, and recent research is reaffirming the impact that leaders have on improving schools. At a time when leadership is critically important, turnover increases, and it is increasingly difficult to attract leaders to the profession. Unlike other professions that provide a developmental incubation period to their leaders, the accountability for educational leaders is the same on their first day as their tenth year. For those currently leading and those interested in leading, this book is a gift that will reward the reader with an understanding and guide that will impact your preparation and practice.

The dictionary defines *contour* as the line which defines a form or edge—an outline. The contour describes the outermost edges of a form, as well as dramatic changes of plane within the form. The authors have outlined educational leadership in a masterful way and have provided a descriptive view of the dramatic changes within. While reading this book, I frequently reflected on how perceptive and insightful the authors were in describing the art and practice of educational leadership. Through the pages, the topography that defines the edges combined with the intricacies that emerged provided me a deeper understanding of the complexities of educational leadership.

There are many educational leadership books on the market, and most of them deal with narrow aspects of educational leadership. These books with a topical focus provide consumers with a non-contextually-based issue treatment that may describe the parameters but don't sufficiently depict the dramatic changes that are redefining educational leadership. *Contours of Great Leadership* not only outlines the parameters but drills down into the foundation of what constitutes great educational leadership.

Contours of Great Leadership's destiny isn't to the bookshelf of past reads or the virtual library but to the virtual and physical desktop of daily reference.

Dick Flanary
Deputy Executive Director, Programs and Services
National Association of Secondary School Principals

1

A PRISM FOR UNDERSTANDING GREAT LEADERSHIP

Man is imminently a storyteller. His search for a purpose, a cause, an ideal, a mission and the like is largely a search for a plot and a pattern in the development of his life story—a story that is basically without meaning or pattern. The turning of our lives into a story is also a means of rousing the interest of others in us and associating them with us.

—Eric Hoffer (1955, p. 97)

Human leadership has most likely existed ever since humans have been around the planet. Humans are social animals. And when speech, and with it language as symbolic capital, became a defining feature of human activity, leadership assumed the capability of being put into ideas, concepts, and words. And those words became the means to motivate, mold, warn, or sell, in short, the linkage between the world of words and actions, and the bond and bridges between leaders and followers.

And it should likewise be clear that leadership is an exercise in social power. Any discussion of leadership has to be *interactional* because it involves an exchange and the construction of a bond between those who lead and those who follow, or perhaps more accurately, those who bestow upon leaders their approval and thereby empower them to lead.

That some who stepped forward were better at it than others was obvious. The effectiveness of leaders has been anchored in:

- Their capability to give life to shared visions and unite people in a common cause, common enemy, or a common fate even when strenuous effort was a requirement and the likelihood of immediate results was not a reality;
- The force of their ideas and causes that could attract and retain those who shared or came to share in the leader's agenda;
- The times and the circumstances, that is, the immediate contexts in which leaders and followers were embedded and engaged in a common struggle or activity; and
- The creation of hope, the existence of a common destiny which requires common action.

So leaders swim in culture and symbols, they seek to propel others to give them social power manifested ultimately in political power inside and/ or outside institutions. Leaders must understand how to create communal cohesion, first in belief and then in the construction of a common activity or outcome. And they must work to maintain that cohesion by speaking to shared aspirations or fears of their common group. They serve as beacons pointing the way, guiding group activity and pointing out what activities or actions result in the desired outcomes and which ones do not.

They thus serve as a disciplinarian, sometimes with coercive powers and sometimes only with moral authority. When a leader is able to coalesce with followers on a mass scale then the magnitude of their accomplishments is similarly multiplied. This result was noted by Jawaharlal Nehru when he said, "Great leaders have something in them which inspires a whole people and makes them do great deeds" (Brussell, 1988, p. 317).

THE NATURE OF EDUCATIONAL LEADERSHIP

While leadership is a human proclivity in all realms, the construction of leaders, we believe it is an entirely constructed phenomenon, though not deterministic, but constrained and shaped by the times, the culture, and the modes of communication which govern human actions in context. And there is nothing in our work which suggests that one could or would eliminate the entirely idiosyncratic and utter uniqueness of those who become our leaders in schools or in other realms.

Having said this, the nature of educational leadership is further constrained by those individuals who occupy formal positions in educational institutions and organizations such as schools or colleges. Leaders can and do exist outside such institutional arrangements. Even though some scholars (Nielsen, 2004) argue for "leaderless organizations" based on the idea that rank-based thinking (working in a hierarchy of roles) promotes manipulation, corruption, and the abuse of power (Blasé & Blasé, 2003), we see little evidence that organizations will be leaderless, especially not in the current culture of accountability.

However, the individuals who comprise our focus occupy such offices, and these are further constraints to what they can do, perhaps even to say or think within them. Educational leadership is therefore an activity which exists within:

- A formal structure, most often a bureaucracy or an organization with bureaucratic structure and functions;
- Defined, though not necessarily confined (at least in an ability to influence others) to a role set within a hierarchy of other roles;
- Most often constrained by a social purpose which is highly conservative, controlled by cultural elites who prefer the socioeconomic status quo to any change which would threaten their socioeconomic position or that of their children;
- Modes of communication which must fit within bureaucratic expectations, contractual and legalistic agreements, contracts, and regulations and prevailing federal and/or state laws;
- Cultural mores and norms that are neither universal nor diverse in nature, but reflect and reinforce the culture of the "haves" and the way they communicate with one another as well as language, style, manners, dress;
- A semiautonomous work force which retains, despite increasing attempts to regulate and control it, considerable leeway in determining the type and kind of work performed in the classroom, the essential workplace in the schools, and who, by joint action and other internal and external means, blunt or negate administrative directives for change, positive or negative;

- A political arena which is very close to the people who are served or touched by the institution and who, via the mechanisms of local democracy and political influence, interfere with and influence the operations of the enterprise including leading efforts to replace leaders and/or workers the majority find objectionable to their interests or immediate political agendas.

In short, educational leadership is about politics, politics, politics. Politics is the art of influence and the means to extend that influence in the various work realms of the school.

Those realms involve technical aspects of the core activity of schools, namely, teaching and learning; systems of support to teaching and learning; the distribution of resources and the procedures employed to obtain and distribute them; the means to assess and change procedures so that the desired results they are employed to attain are improved, however defined. Other realms include the establishment and maintenance of a work climate in which human growth and development is connected to work improvement, and there is respect for the dignity and humanity of all concerned, which means that there is a minimum of fear present.

A MODEL TO DISCUSS EDUCATIONAL LEADERSHIP

The model of educational leadership which frames this book and our research about it is a derivative of Shaffer's (2009) epistemic network analysis. Shaffer's work is about designing digital learning environments which are rich enough to deal with contextual variables. He is concerned with evidence-centered design of which central to that effort is "the idea of alignment between learning theory and assessment method, between evidence and hypothesized mechanisms of thinking and learning in a given arena" (p. 2).

Shaffer's work centers on the notion that a community of practice possesses a culture (Rhode & Shaffer, 2004) which has a kind of grammar, that is, a skeleton composed of skills, knowledge, values, identity, and an epistemology. *Identity* is the way members of the community of practice see themselves. *Epistemology* is validating some perspectives or claims as compatible within the community of practice and invalidating or ignoring other perspectives or claims.

We adapted this model to more logically fit our work. We liked very much the notion of a *community of practice* and we agree that such a community does possess a frame or paradigm (to use an older term) by which some actions are considered appropriate and others are not. The frame also is the platform by which conversations about practice are held.

However, perhaps because our work is leadership centered, we determined that identity was not on the same plane as the notion of skills, knowledges, and values, but that identity was the result of them. Thus, we elevated identity to a different position, and this is shown in figure 1.1.

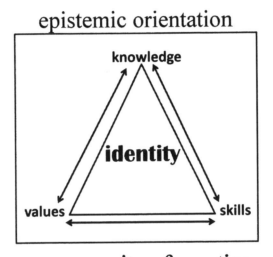

Figure 1.1.   Educational Leadership as Performance in Context

Further, we took the perspective that identity is never static and that it has many layers and faces. In short it is co-constructed and interactional with knowledge, skills, and values, and this interaction occurs with an epistemic frame which is constructed itself and which exercises a governing function which confines and defines the nature of a community of professional practice (Lumby & English, 2009).

It is within the concept of a community of practice within an educational institutional framework that our notion of "great leadership" is located. It should be explained that "great" leadership is not an endorsement of the traditional idea of "heroic" leadership, the proffered mythological comic book figure riding into chaos and restoring order and productivity, such as Batman or Superman. Khurana (2002) studied how corporations made huge mistakes in hiring their CEOs following that image:

> The myth of the charismatic CEO disguises this inconvenient reality. The charismatic illusion is fostered by tales of white knights, lone rangers, and other such heroic figures whose origins lie in the fairy tales that serve a child's need to feel protected from the world's dangers. (p. 208)

Khurana (2002) succinctly nailed his research down when he said, "No single individual can save an organization" (p. 209). We believe, and our research and others show, that "great" leadership is not only distributive but collaborative.

THE FLUID NATURE OF IDENTITY

The key to great leadership is identity. For being a constant in an otherwise emergent field, identity itself is constantly being negotiated within the field in which it is operating. John Heywood (2005) put it this way:

> The ability to function in social groups of all kinds requires an understanding of self as we move within a plurality of social systems. It is a two-way process, attitudes and values feed into the societal process as well as the other way round, and groups take on their own identity and create their own culture. (pp. 44–45)

The dynamic we are describing is shown in figure 1.2, the identity continua. This schematic shows that identity is interactive with values, knowledge, and skills and is on a *continua* of development. What this means is that leaders grow into greatness because becoming a great leader is acquired or as we present the idea that leadership is an *accoutrement*, a personal fabric sewn together over time.

What we learned about great leadership is that leadership is not an independent variable in the equation to the situation in which a leader is located. What this means is that leadership is not static and isolated from where the leader is. For a long time military academies were aimed at studying battlefield commanders to learn the lessons of generalship irrespective of the times and context of the way battles were won or lost.

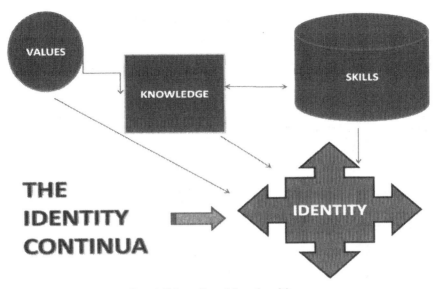

Figure 1.2. Poor to Great Educational Leadership

As in educational administration, military leadership became the province of the behaviorists and the social scientists. But the prescient analyses of the military historian John Keegan (1987) refute this perspective:

> Both are the methods of social scientists and, as with all social science, condemn those who practice them to the agony of making universal and general what is stubbornly local and particular. I am an historian, not a social scientist, and am therefore free to believe that the generalship of one age and place may not at all resemble that of another. Not only am I free thus to believe; I actually do so, and all the more certain after thirty years' practice of my trade. (p. 1)

Keegan (1987) reminds us that the ideas or notions of those considered great from the proclivity to generalize across time and place has resulted in the mistaken notion that great ideas were "commonly portrayed as free-floating in time, simply [from] a mind more powerful than any which had applied itself to its chosen subject before . . . Rarely is either subjected to the rigor of contextualization" (p. 3). Keegan then presciently warns, "Yet context, when theories . . . are at stake, is all" (p. 3).

We can also see the mistakes made in popular books about "great leaders or great companies." Jim Collins's (2001) best-selling book, *Good to*

Great, is an example. After elaborate and ostensibly thorough vetting and poring over many indices, Collins presents his list of eleven companies that his data demonstrate are "great." Obviously for a company to be great there had to be "great" leaders running them.

Collins's (2001) ultimate list of "great companies" included Abbott, Circuit City, Fannie Mae, Gillette, Kimberly-Clark, Kroger, Nucor, Philip Morris, Pitney Bowes, Walgreens, and Wells Fargo. Eleven years later we know that Circuit City

> became the best at implementing the "4-S" model (service, selection, savings, satisfaction) applied to big-ticket consumer sales [and is no longer in business] and Fannie Mae declared [by Collins] to . . . become the best capital markets player in anything that pertains to mortgages. (p. 101)

As for Fannie Mae and Freddie Mac, an editorial in the *Wall Street Journal* (2010) noted that both of these mortgage giants had depended heavily on selling mortgage-backed securities from Countrywide Financial Corporation headed by convicted executive Angelo Mozilo, who was fined $22.5 million. This was the largest such punishment to an executive of a public company, with U.S. taxpayers having to bail out "Fannie and Freddie of $148 billion and counting" (*Wall Street Journal*, 2010, p. A16).

Later the Securities and Exchange Commission filed a civil lawsuit against six former executives at Fannie Mae and Freddie Mac. This lawsuit portends that the "executives knowingly misled investors about the volumes of risky mortgages that the companies were purchasing as the housing boom turned to bust" (Timiraos & Bray, 2011, p. B1).

Likewise, Wells Fargo agreed to pay an $85 million civil penalty for the practice of steering "thousands of potential prime-mortgage borrowers into more costly sub-prime loans" (Simon & McGrane, 2011, p. C3). Ira Rheingold, executive director of the National Association of Consumer Advocates, declared that the action by the feds was "a pretty strong statement about the bad practices Wells Fargo has engaged in [and that it was] a confirmation that these problems were part of the culture of the firm, not the result of a few rogue employees" (Simon & McGrane, 2011, p. C3).

Earlier, Wells Fargo was ordered by a federal judge in California to pay $200 million. Wells Fargo had "to compensate customers who the judge said were improperly charged millions in overdraft fees" (Eckblad, 2010, p. C13).

What these approaches should tell us is leadership is fragile, fluid, interactive, and contingent on context and circumstances. Despite Collins's ostensible detailed tracking of the companies he eventually labeled "great" and put into such a salubrious category, the evidence and data did not produce a permanent "great" company at all. Some slid into oblivion and others engaged in either risky or illegal practices and fell into "great" disrepute.

When contexts and times change, organizations can be severely challenged, and their leaders are likely to be challenged as well. There are few leaders good for all times. Even the great British prime minister Winston Churchill was "dumped from his office by British voters" (Gilbert, 1991, p. 855) after he had been the "rock" which held the country together and faced down the Nazi conquest of Europe, often with only his defiant rhetoric in Parliament and when his field generals were too timid to offer a good fight to the enemy.

We will look at "greatness" in educational leaders as part of a journey they themselves undergo to gain a better understanding of themselves, as well as working within and then transcending the contexts in which they find themselves. Great educational leaders are masters of bureaucracy. They understand organizations and the people in them. Above all, they rarely rest on their laurels because they understand so well that success must be attained every day and is not some permanent oasis free from the trials and challenges because of their good past efforts.

THE NATURE OF *ACCOUTREMENTS*

The research that undergirds this book began in 1999 and produced the book *Leadership on Purpose: Promising Practices for African American and Hispanic Students* (Papa [Papalewis] & Fortune, 2002). The most recent iteration of this research has been with Arizona superintendents and principals with a team of researchers (see chapter 6 and appendix B). Both groups, through surveys and focus groups, have been asked to identify practices they viewed as critical to high achieving students in communities with high poverty and diversity.

That research has led to what have been defined as the *accoutrements* of leadership (English, Papa, Mullen, & Creighton, 2012; Papa, 2011; Papa, 2011, May; Papa & English, 2011). These are outlined below:

- *Leading Adult Learners:* Leaders should know adult learners *learn* on a need-to-know basis.

- *Understanding Human Agency:* Leaders must have a varied reper- toire of fair and just behaviors.
- *Awareness of Ignored Intended Skills:* Leaders must be adept at lis- tening, mentoring, and showing compassion.
- *Strong Intellectual Curiosity:* A leader is curious. Curiosity is fairness in action as it asks "why" with no assigning of blame.
- *Knowledge of Futurity:* Leaders must be exposed to learning frames that go against the grain of current wisdom. Going against the grain may just be the best leader trait we can encourage.
- *Imaginativeness:* Creativity, inspiration, originality, resourcefulness, visionary, artistic, inventive, ingenious are the synonyms to imagina- tive leadership. Experience with good heart, an almost spiritual need to be of service for others; to be the hope for others; to help others be all they can be; to see the good in others is limited only by one's lack of imagination. (Papa, 2011, May, p. 69)

These *accoutrements* go beyond the basic requirements of a leader's posi- tion. These are those *special characteristics and skills* that through applica- tion and practice are sewn into one's persona. These are the accessories that separate the great leaders from functional to poor leaders. They are rooted in the leader's identity, his or her orientation and competence within the context and culture of a special kind of institutional space, the school.

Distinguishing mediocre to functional to great leadership is the focus of this book. Empirical research over a fourteen-year period led to identify- ing effective leadership characteristics called *accoutrements* (see chapter 6 for full description of the research). Who the school leader is and what the leader does matters. These are those *special characteristics and skills* that the leaders of high achieving schools possess and actively display which lead to high achieving students and programs.

We take note of other important research conducted by Hallinger and Heck (2011) on attempting to determine how leadership actually leads to school improvement. They tested four models over a four-year period within 198 primary schools in the United States. These models were:

1. The Direct Effects Model—in this model the leadership of the school is seen as the primary "driver" for improvements in student learning;
2. The Mediated Effects Model—in this model leadership prompts growth in student achievement by increasing the schools' capacity for improvement;

3. The Reversed Mediated Effects Model—in this paradigm changes in student growth then prompt a change in the capacity of the school toward improvement and enhanced leadership;
4. The Reciprocal Effects Model—in this construct leadership and school improvement capacities are seen as mutually influential, which leads to student growth.

The results of Hallinger and Heck's research indicated that model 1, the Direct Effects Model, sometimes called the "heroic leadership" model, did not yield significant effects in reading or math. In model 2, the Mediated Effects construct indicated that "collaborative leadership was positively related to change in school capacity [and] a change in school improvement capacity positively affected growth in math" (p. 479). In addition, the researcher saw a "small, positive *indirect* relationship between changes in collaborative leadership and growth in student learning in reading and math" (p. 479).

Consequently, a testing of model 3 did not indicate it worked. It did not serve as a stimulant for change in either school improvement capacity or collaborative leadership. In contrast, model 4 was a very strong indicator that collaborative leadership was strongly related to school improvement capacity and to student growth. Hallinger and Heck (2011) conclude by observing, "Our test of Model 4, therefore, supported the proposition that changes in collaborative leadership and school improvement capacity are mutually reinforcing processes" (p. 479).

One of the main lessons from the Hallinger and Heck (2011) study is one which is reinforced by our *accoutrements* leadership model, that is, that "from the perspective of leadership practice, the research supports the view that school improvement leadership is highly contextualized" (p. 482). Furthermore, this research also supports our view that the school "culture" is a critical variable, so important that Hallinger and Heck (2011) noted that "the impact of the school's culture on leadership was greater than vice versa" (p. 482).

The Critical Questions in School Culture

Stoll and Fink (1996) have identified the cultural norms in a school that are connected to school improvement. These have been extrapolated and are shown in table 1.1.

Table I.I.   The Critical Dimensions of School Culture

Dimension	Content	Key Indicator
Shared goals	A common goal and future are held by all members of the school which provides everyone with a way to assess individual and group efforts.	*We know where we are going.*
Responsibility for success	There is a shared belief that all children can learn and no pupil is excused because of their background or family circumstances.	*We must succeed.*
Collegiality	Based on more than common stories, but actual joint work which consists of action research, team teaching, mentoring, and peer coaching.	*We are working together.*
Continuous improvement	The feeling that no matter how good the school is, it can be improved. This is based on a healthy skepticism of the status quo.	*We can get better.*
Lifelong learning	The belief that learning never ceases and that adults must be learning alongside the students.	*Learning is for everyone.*
Risk taking	This involves the feeling that failing after trying a new idea or technique is okay. The leader models risk-taking behavior.	*We learn by trying something new.*
Support	This involves giving time to others, making oneself personally available to others to listen and care about them.	*There is always someone there to help.*
Mutual respect	Groupthink is discouraged, a lack of status consciousness prevails, opportunities for newcomers to be heard, where tolerance and sympathy are present.	*Everyone has something to offer.*
Openness	Criticism is not discouraged but is recognized as essential for growth and development.	*We can discuss our differences.*
Celebration and humor	Teachers and students feel valued. Humor reduces tension and creates a sense of belonging.	*We feel good about ourselves.*

Bourdieu's Concept of Reflexivity vs. Reflective Thinking

Understanding the difference between *reflexive versus reflective thinking* is central to solid educational advancement. The notion of reflexivity is one of the hallmarks of Pierre Bourdieu's work. This is not a common word in the lexicon of most educators.

The more common concept among educators is that of *reflection*, which has a long history beginning with John Dewey's *Experience and Education*, released in 1938. More recently many books have been written about reflection in education (see, for example, Clift, Houston, & Pugach, 1990; Loughran, 1996; Osterman & Kottkamp, 1993; Schon, 1983, 1987; York-Barr, Sommers, Ghere, & Montie, 2001).

More Than "Reflective Evaluation Craft"

Many educators experience reflective practice as simply knowledge of your performance, whether in the classroom or otherwise. And so it would involve what Schon (1987) described as "knowledge in action" (p. 49), which may employ *tacit knowledge* as situations are recognized in which past experiences can be applied. The definition of *tacit knowledge* begins with "the fact that we can know more than we can tell" (Polanyi, 1967, p. 4).

Research on tacit knowledge undertaken by Nestor-Baker and Hoy (2001) showed that reputationally successful school superintendents in Ohio (n = 22) indicated that they

> commented repeatedly that reflection on self, on the problems at hand, and on the profession in general causes them to hone in on the undercurrents of problems, helping them to generate avenues for action. In their own ways, they were saying that reflection focused on general or specific goals helps to create tacit knowledge. (p. 126)

Bringing *tacit knowledge* into awareness is one of the functions of *reflective thinking*.

Van Manen (1977) has identified three levels of reflective thinking. They are (1) *technical reflection*, which centers on the processes, methods, and/or skills required to attain established goals or objectives; (2) *practical reflection*, which also focuses on methods but in relationship to predetermined goals and sorts the values behind whether the goals are really desirable; and (3) *critical reflection*, which is centered on the ethical, moral, or social value of a particular practice and which asks questions pertaining to whether a practice promotes equity or diversity.

Using Van Manen's (1977) delineation we can see the kinds of reflection involved in the following example:

Sample technical reflective questions

1. Is collaborative student learning the best way to teach students to work with one another?
2. What kind of curricular format best promotes alignment?
3. What is the most appropriate way to initiate professional learning communities?
4. What administrative skills are most useful in improving a school's climate?

Sample practical reflective questions

1. What form of strategic planning will enable us to define the most important goals for our school?
2. How can we sort our goals to create greater diversity among our teaching cadre?
3. What budgetary practices and procedures will enable us to distribute our resources more equitably?
4. How does the current curriculum configuration incorporate the arts in a meaningful way and improve curricular balance?

Sample critically reflective questions

1. How do the current grouping practices promote social coherence and equity?
2. What are the moral and ethical issues if we close the schools in the poorest part of our district and bus those students elsewhere?
3. If we increase time-on-task for the lowest performing students and cut their access to the humanities, how will they acquire a well-rounded education?
4. Our Advanced Placement classes are dominated by our upper class white students. How do we increase enrollment among our students of color?

Bourdieu's concept of *reflexivity* (1999) is much deeper than any of these *reflective* questions. The difference is shown in figure 1.3. The number 1 in this schematic shows a perceiver/thinker considering what actions should be taken within a given context. Most often these are related to a goal or objective such as increased student learning or increased personal capacities or renewing "clarity of personal and professional purpose" (York-Barr, Sommers, Ghere, & Montie, 2001, p. 13).

Number 2 in figure 1.3 shows reflective thinking that involves "knowledge in action," a phrase used by Schon (1987, p. 49) to describe *reflective practice*. Osterman and Kottkamp (1993) also support Schon's concept by remarking, "Professionals engage in reflective practice to develop a new awareness of their own performance and to improve the quality of their practice" (p. ix). But this distinction is not Bourdieu's concept of *reflexivity*.

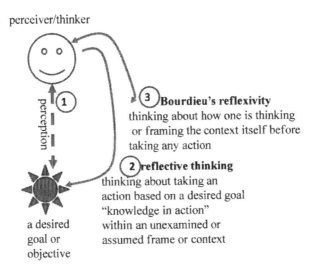

Figure 1.3. Bourdieu's Concept of Reflexivity vs. Reflective Thinking

Bourdieu (1999) asked, "How can we claim to engage in the scientific investigations of presuppositions if we do not work to gain knowledge of our own presuppositions?" (p. 608). The difference, he said, was between a science that knows of its own constructions and one that does not. To put that into an individual's sphere of action would mean a perceiver/thinker who understood his/her own presuppositions and one who did not.

Deer (2008) based on Bourdieu indicates for a perceiver attempting to engage in *reflexive thinking* is a struggle to "recognize their own objective position within the intellectual and academic field" (p. 201). In other words, the perceiver has to force himself/herself to come to grips with how his/her own unconscious thought processes color the object he/she may be perceiving.

An Example of Reflexivity: Rational Choice Theory as a Silent Presupposition

An example of reflexive thinking in practice would be to analyze what the perceiver has assumed "should be" at work, that is, the kind of *tacit knowledge* that is held unconsciously. For example, English and Bolton (2008) discerned in their interviews of middle line managers in the United States and England that even at the middle tier of bureaucratic levels administrative decision makers engaged in autonomous actions from the larger organization when their own values were at odds with them, but they were not always thought out ahead of time.

They found instead that these middle line managers were more event or context connected to levels of risk and situational uncertainty. The process of reflexive thinking would be to bring them into conscious awareness.

Now let us return to the questions posed under the three levels (technical, practical, and critical) reflective questions from Van Manen (1977). In the way the questions are framed one can perceive a silent narrative. That frame echoes *rational choice theory* or RCT. Rational choice theory is based on the assumption that "all human behavior can be viewed as involving participants who maximize their utility for a stable set of preferences and accumulate an optimal amount of information and other inputs in a variety of [situations] markets" (Becker, 1976, p. 8).

The key to maximization as Bohman (1992) explains is "consistency" (p. 210). For maximization to occur a situation must be stable and provide a consistent set of constraints and possibilities. And "maximization requires that a rational agent acts to achieve the best consequences and thus chooses the highest ranking alternative among the set of feasible actions and strategies" (Bohman, 1992, p. 210).

For example, take the very first technical question, "Is collaborative student learning the best way to teach students to work with one another?" To answer this question one would have to have some knowledge of *all the ways* one could teach students to work with one another. Then one would have to have some test in which "best" was determined. How would one measure which one was "best"? The solution or answer to the question is solved by acquiring more information. Under those conditions comes an answer.

In the second tier of questions (practical), number 3 asks, "What budgetary practices and procedures will enable us to distribute our resources more equitably?" To answer this question one would have to know about a great number of budgetary practices and how they work. Then there would have to be a definition of what was meant by "equitable." Then each budgetary practice would have to be weighed against this criterion. In each of these examples, the assumption is that the decision maker is rational and only interested in objective analyses and the search for an optimal answer.

So what's wrong with a rational choice model for practice? The problem with these conditions is that there is "no place for stupidity, ignorance, or herd behavior" (Cassidy, 2009, p. 102). Similarly, rational choice theory and its derivative in economics are called *the efficient market hypothesis.* That hypothesis "assumes transparent self-knowledge in order to maximize our self-interests, [and] we must know what they are" (Cassidy, 2009, p. 204). And, as Cassidy (2009) notes, "even if [people] sit down and try to calculate all the pros and cons of a certain purchase, or investment, the figures rarely give an unequivocal answer" (p. 204).

Reflective practice in this way asks us to identify an issue with our practice and to plan to remedy it, whereas applying Bourdieu's *reflexivity* means stepping outside of the prevailing logic box of preferences based on assumptions in which both the question and the answer are embedded. It is more than being perceptive. Figure 1.3 shows what is involved with Bourdieu's concept of *reflexivity.* Bourdieu believed that "action in terms of explicitly posed goals, or consciously posited ends is . . . an illusion" (Grenfell, 2007, p. 203). It is a continuous process and never-ending quest for the individual to pursue.

The ensuing chapters in this book are examples of (a) reflective thinking and then (b) reflexive thinking. For experience to work within the concept of leadership as *accoutrements,* the authors of this book have worked at both levels in revealing the matter of identity which lies behind great leadership in the schools.

CHAPTER LEARNING EXTENSIONS

Each chapter in this book ends with this section, chapter learning extensions, as it is our attempt to test your understandings of both what has been delivered in the chapter by the authors and your reflections and thoughts to help you in your critical analyses of the lenses you apply. This chapter has focused on the nature and effectiveness of leadership and proposes a model as a means to construct one's *identity continua* of leadership.

Testing Your Understanding of This Chapter about Great Leaders

Look over the matrix in table 1.2. Remember that your response should be two-edged, that is, how it looks gazing through the lens of the chapter and then a second skeptical examination of the lens itself.

Table 1.2. What Do You Believe about Great Leaders?

Great leader statements	What do you think? True/false? Yes/no?	Where you are in your understanding
1.1. Leadership is constructed by oneself.		
1.2. One's identity is one's own perception.		
1.3. Leadership is reflective thinking.		
1.4. Leadership is reflexive knowledge.		
1.5. Distributed leadership is the answer to models of heroic leadership.		

2

HABITS OF REFLECTION AND FOCUS ON INSTRUCTION

If you want to build a ship, don't drum up people to collect wood and don't assign them tasks and work, but rather teach them to long for the endless immensity of the sea.

—Antoine de Saint-Exupéry (1900–1944)

We have discussed how our values impact our skills and knowledge, and how we are impacted by the same. Sometimes, we may be so consumed with the fact that we are *able* to do something that we fail to stop and think if we *should* do it. That is the role our values play on our knowledge and our skills.

When we examine today's political scene, it is understandable why so many aspiring educational leaders shun the concept of values altogether. The very term construes images of career politicians slinging mud at their opponents, or bending the rules to suit their own personal needs. There is no lack of scandal in the political realm; it's no wonder a value-minded individual would want to avoid politics.

But, by our definition of politics as the art of influence, and the means to extend that influence as noted in chapter 1, an educational leader must master the political arts. The key to this is fundamentally one's values. The corruption so evident in governmental politicians can be directly traced back to the core of what drives their decisions. The driving force behind seeking leadership positions shades all leadership actions. If that force is the desire for personal gain, leaders use the power inherent in their position to serve themselves, rather than to serve the students and the institution.

MATURATION OF LEADERSHIP

It seems the general belief in the United States that public schools are failing the American people. Continual waves of school reform crash upon the shores of education, most designed without the benefit of any educators in the mix. Attempts to "turn around" failing schools (Papa & English, 2011) lead to new frustrations on the part of the schools and society. Few turnaround efforts are successful, and the one common thread found in most successful turnaround schools is the quality of the school leaders (Brady, 2003; Papa & English, 2011). What kind of leadership do those leaders possess that others overlook?

Robert Greenleaf's 1970 essay called for servant-first leadership, which puts the needs of others as priority, unlike leader-first behavior, which strives for personal power and possessions. Participative leadership is not necessarily democratic, but rather allows for "opportunity and responsibility of having a say in your job, to have influence over the management of organizational resources based on your own competence and your willingness to accept problem ownership" (DePree, 1989, p. 48).

Best leadership comes from removing obstacles from the group to help them reach their goals. Not the desire to make a name for oneself, but rather to secure the success of one's school, makes an educational leader great. A continual maturation process of habitual reflection and honest self-assessment leads to an acceptance of capacities and limitations, allowing for the establishment of supportive, trusting relationships with others, based on the core value of continual growth and improvement.

In developing these relationships among one's school, we see the continual maturation of leadership, coordinating collaboration throughout the community, by capitalizing on the strengths of each individual. The same common set of values, knowledge, and skills that combine to make one's school function highly, impact the school's interaction with its community in the same manner.

When the school functions harmoniously, all members are able to build effective relationships with parents and the greater school community because of that internal balance. When we replace valuing power with valuing service, our knowledge and skills become dedicated to the ideal of service to others, to the school, and to society (Culver, 2009).

One of the highest-regarded characteristics of great leadership is honesty. When leaders are honest with themselves, and their followers, about their capacity and limitation, they demonstrate a commitment to a process of continual growth on the job, and a respect for human dignity. Rather than wasting energy in fostering a false image of perfection, a true leader values reflection, assessment, adjustment, and a continuous loop of improvement beginning with their own. Morrill (2007) calls this contextual leadership. Humility is necessary for a school leader to consistently seek information prior to decision making, foster collaboration, and help others develop as leaders.

SHARED LEADERSHIP

Sharing leadership can be difficult to adjust to, for individuals who have been successful in carrying a heavy workload. As novice leaders, they may fear becoming micromanagers, or worse, failing to achieve a goal. Trusting and enabling the team to work toward the common goal, and removing obstacles to that accomplishment, become the primary role of a servant-first leader (Greenleaf, 1970).

By developing leadership at all levels and nurturing collaboration, a great leader opens their school to the level of expertise of *all* of the staff. Rather than limiting the school to the limits of only the leader's knowledge and skills, they place a high value on open communication, continual learning, and shared leadership.

In order to channel the energy necessary to build and maintain a highly effective school, the leader must find a way to affect the heart of each member of the school. They must establish a safe environment for these members to collaborate, lead, and experiment without fear. Negativity and adversity must be replaced with a search for solutions through collaboration founded in shared belief that the students come first. Determination of where to allocate funds is a process that can divide faculty, staff, and administration.

In a culture of putting students first, resources are distributed to improve student achievement. Trust in each other allows all concerned parties to communicate effectively to decide what is necessary for that improvement. When you put your money where your mouth is, and do whatever it takes to make students successful, those entrusted with it must demonstrate accountability for that trust. Accountability to peers may be one of the greatest demonstrations of student-first mentality.

FOCUS ON INSTRUCTION

One of the most critical values a school leader should hold dear is superior instruction. The outstanding leader will protect instruction time, provide the highest quality of professional development, and model the strategies they expect teachers to practice. When you curtail classroom interruptions, and hold off announcements for noninstructional moments, you demonstrate respect for instruction and instructors. When you keep staff meetings and professional development sessions separate, you demonstrate the value you place on instruction.

By applying the very art and science of exceptional teaching you expect in every classroom to your professional development sessions, you are modeling your knowledge, skills, and value of teaching and learning. Customizing professional development to meet the school's needs and those of individual teachers requires competent collaboration of teachers and administrators, a common instructional language and common goals, examination of data to select objectives for individual sessions, and at least a yearlong plan.

Approaching professional development with the same drive you want your teachers to demonstrate in their classroom helps to establish your reputation and respect as an instructional leader. And most importantly, it is the right and moral way to lead.

School leaders who choose to value the illusion of power and control over their faculty and staff will find themselves at the mercy of that faculty and staff. If the team accepts the direction the leader points them in, they will follow. If they reject it, there is little more to be said.

To successfully serve as an instructional leader, a culture of empowered teacher-leaders must be developed. When an administrator makes the time to be in the classroom on a regular basis, and truly knows the strengths and needs of each teacher on campus, they can coach their outstanding teachers to be coaches to other teachers. Demonstrating their dedication to premier instruction, the leader spreads that value through an ever-growing core of teacher-leaders.

A powerful web of high expectations is built as proficient teachers are recognized for their skills and are recruited to model for, and coach, developing teachers. It is through building high expectations for instruction that the peer pressure to excel sets the culture of instruction on a campus. No leader can do this alone; they must develop leadership throughout every level by demonstrating their respect for teaching and learning.

Having a school faculty and staff interact positively with parents and the school community is an ideal situation that may seem overwhelming if isolation is the culture of the school. When significant culture barriers exist between teachers and parents, simple school-home communication can be stymied. Is it too ideal to expect teachers to communicate with parents when they don't speak the same language? While on the topic of idealism, can we truly expect all students to learn? Is that realistic? To school districts in this study and the years of research that has preceded (Papa [Papalewis] & Fortune, 2002), yes, we can expect it, and yes, it is realistic!

What is it that allows some schools to break down any barriers between them and success for all students? They hold strong to optimism. Yes, what others put off as too idealistic, too pie-in-the-sky, too unrealistic, these school districts achieve because they don't accept the alternative. Each leader, each individual connected to the district, believes in doing the impossible, when necessary, to make every individual student successful. There is no single blueprint for making reality ideal; the secret to each school, each community, is held within the creativity of that school community. By learning and working together, with a can-do attitude, it is possible!

A constant value expressed by leaders in the school districts most recently interviewed (see chapter 6 and appendix B) is the power of teamwork. Free-flowing communication was touted as paramount to their success. Superintendents had open-door policies. District experts were on call for building personnel. Communication moved from the bottom up, and from the top down, keeping everyone informed and part of the team.

Collaboration is not a buzzword in these districts; it is their roadmap. Through sharing data; holding deep, meaningful conversations; and removing any barriers to sharing resources (including personal energy through coaching, and even rolling up sleeves and pitching in), exceptional districts walk their talk and clearly demonstrate the value they place on teamwork.

The core activities of schools, as stated prior, include teaching and learning and the systems of support for those, distribution of resources, and the ability to measure and change procedures to improve desired results. These functions are supported by a work environment focused on professional development for improved job performance, and mutual respect.

School leaders who are successful in coordinating these activities share a common trilogy of values, which channel their knowledge into the application of their skills toward their desired outcomes. This trilogy consists of placing high value on the art and science of instruction, idealism, and teamwork.

HANDS-ON INSTRUCTIONAL LEADERSHIP

Effective school leaders make instruction the number-one priority in their schools. When an organization fails to perform its primary purpose, that organization is certain to fail; it ceases to exist. The primary purpose of schools is to educate students, and that is done through effective curriculum and instruction. We have found the consistent value in effective school leadership to be the importance of instruction. They know the importance of using data in their decision making. More importantly, they apply that knowledge by developing leadership at all levels of their schools and districts.

Teams of teachers and administrators work collaboratively in continuous assessment of curriculum, determining if the outcomes of the curriculum "hit" the target. These teams speak the same curricular language, and continually compare outcome data to the curriculum to determine the effectiveness of their instructional plan. If, at each level, students are achieving the desired learning results, as measured by predetermined assessments, the team has an effective curriculum.

When there is a smooth flow of student development from year to year, the team has achieved curricular continuity. Our effective school leaders encourage, develop, measure, and inspire these teams in this continuous loop of reflective development and implementation of curriculum planning.

At this point, you may be thinking that valuing curriculum and instruction is enough. Leading this process includes scheduling plenty of collaborative "team" time and providing a fair dose of cheerleading to the task, right? Not exactly.

Despite popular myth, teaching is not for "those who can't." Teaching is a highly specialized skill, based on hitting a moving target of ever-evolving outcomes, with ever-variant resources. Students don't come by preset specification; we work with what we have, and therein lies the art to the science of teaching. So, what does this have to do with the leadership of teachers? Because school leaders must be the *principal teachers*! If you expect your teachers to make a difference to their students, you must first make a difference to your teachers. Period! If you want the teachers' attention, you must earn their respect and trust.

What we have found in all outstanding school leaders was a huge value for instructional leadership. They all knew, and could *teach* the curriculum in their schools, and the teachers *knew* it! How did the teachers know this? Quite simply, because they *saw* it. Principals, curriculum directors, personnel directors, and superintendents: all were seen regularly, as active instructors, in the classrooms of their schools. They taught the teachers through in-services and through team teaching.

They were no strangers to the teachers or the students. Through their modeling of curricular knowledge and instructional expertise, they earned the respect of their teachers *and* they intimately knew the abilities of those teachers from this close interaction.

Again, this effective model of hands-on faculty development is centered on the shared importance placed on instruction as the primary leadership function of a school and district. From the hiring process, through teacher induction, and on to continual, lifelong learning, highly effective school leaders are highly involved in each step along the way.

It was not unusual for superintendents to interview each employee before the final job offer was made. Rather than viewing this as micromanaging and mistrust of principals' and personnel directors' skills, these highly functioning districts saw this as ultimate dedication to the importance of getting the right "fit" for the districts' vision and mission. In taking the time to discuss the districts' values with each employee, these superintendents demonstrated the values of the district, emphasizing the fundamental necessities of working for their community.

This up-front approach of communicating clear expectations, and alignment of core values, saved the future employee and the district any heartache down the line resulting from a poor "fit" for the job. Individuals with compatible drive, dedication, and yes, values were screened and hired. Those without were redirected elsewhere.

Thus begins the establishment of a common language among district personnel, which ties them together in a common journey, with a common purpose . . . to educate the young people entrusted to them. But it is only the beginning.

Leaders at every level in the district share the responsibility of developing the new hire into a dedicated, highly functional member of the team. These outstanding leaders walk their talk through this process. Because of the value they place on instruction, these leaders find a way to schedule time out of the office so they can interactively coach teachers in the classroom.

This value pushes these leaders to put the time and money into establishing and maintaining effective teacher induction programs and continuous professional development. One leader is not enough to create the common vocabulary necessary to drive the teamwork to make schools effective. Developing neophytes into master teachers, and master teachers into instructional leaders, depends on a culture of community and common purpose. It requires a dedication to lifelong learning, which in turn models the very purpose of schooling.

Highly effective school districts are effective because they are fulfilling their primary function, educating the students entrusted to their care. The common language each district develops to further this function is more than a by-product of this process; it is one of the driving forces behind it. Sharing a common language is fundamental in developing, implementing, and assessing curriculum. It is paramount in discussing student and school data for making decisions.

The common language allows all school community members to be on the same foot, from the students, teachers, support staff, and into the community. Students learn the common language and take on personal leadership in their own education because they can communicate about their learning with their teachers. Through application of their common language to deeper discussions and more meaningful dialogue teachers grow and develop. Professional development meetings take on higher ends due to the shared meanings of district vocabulary. Parents "get" what teachers are talking about in parent-teacher meetings, phone calls, notes, and yes, even override appeals.

The business of education is to invest in people. Effective leaders value that investment. They exude the sense that there is absolutely no ceiling on learning, for anyone. They encourage students, teachers, and communities to share tools and techniques for learning. This collaboration does not disvalue the importance of healthy competition, however. Effective leaders exhibit a very healthy competition, but its focus is not on being better than others. It is focused on being better than they were, in a never-ending spiral of continual improvement.

Students, teachers, school leaders, and school communities are "bit and infected" with the urge for incessant growth. Great leaders clearly model lifelong learning through targeted reading, independent and group study, and reflective assessment. As models for learning, their own assessment and professional growth is overt, and no stranger to 360-degree evaluation. They set the example for healthy self-competition, designing their development to their professional needs and those of their school or district.

This model carries through to the professional development of each school, as flexibility is provided for each school to design a professional development plan to meet its own needs. Again, this growth is overt. The common language of the school and the district again come into play through the assessment of professional development. The data provided through student assessment and personnel evaluations steers future decisions on professional development. To value instruction above all other functions of a school requires more than lip service; it takes concentrated action from all.

OPTIMISM

When interviewing highly effective school leadership teams, one can summarize their attitudes in a single word: optimistic. We are talking 100 percent pure Pollyanna enthusiasm for what they do. Unlike the freshman sense from Education 101, unfounded, untested optimism, these leaders have stood the test of time and practice, weathered political, societal, and cultural storms, and are as positive as Molly McSunshine. Is this unrealistic? Perhaps not, but it is hard to argue with success.

We are taught from our very first education class that "all students can learn," but without the right kind of support, it doesn't take long before many begin to doubt it. Districts composed of great leaders take that belief one step further, and that may be the key to bringing this adage to fruition. They believe "everyone can learn," thus throwing themselves as well as all adults in the system into the mix. In doing so, they take on the belief that "nothing can't be done!" By working and learning together, they somehow find *their* solutions to *their* problems.

We mentioned earlier that great superintendents double-check every employee prior to hiring them. The purpose of this is to make the expectations of the district clear to the employee and see if they share the same values as these winning districts.

Quite simply, highly effective districts believe that "nothing can't be done," "everything is possible," and most importantly, they "don't settle" for less than success for all their children. Because these exceptional superintendents are ultimately responsible for that success, they are looking for people who will "give 200 percent," who "choose excellence," and have a "can-do attitude." Only when the whole team, from the very top to the very bottom, believes that they can make a positive difference to each and every child, can the undoable be done.

These hand-picked employees are "world class"and they know it. They are proud of it, and that fires their ambition to reach every child and truly do whatever it takes in order to make them succeed. They share core values with their leaders, and the school board has earned the trust of those in the "trenches" . . . only there *are* no trenches. The board, superintendent, principals, and department/team leaders put their money where their mouth is; they expect the best, and they remove obstacles in the way.

Each leader values the title of "instructional leader" and proves it in every action. From their knowledge and skills in teaching, to their ability to manipulate the length of the school day or school year (Papa [Papalewis] & Fortune, 2002), these leaders put more time and more resources wherever is necessary.

So, how do these educators differ from those neophytes in Education 101? Both are idealistic. Both are dripping with optimism. Both believe they can change the world and save hundreds and thousands of students. What differs is great educators stand the test of time. They have faced obstacles and found their way around them. Like Captain Kirk and the Kobayashi Maru Starfleet test (EKR, October 2, 2011), they don't accept the "no-win" situation. They live the motto "No shame, no blame, and no excuses." Everyone succeeds. Everyone.

WORKING TOGETHER

Now that we've revealed the *glass half full* intrinsic nature of the men and women who turn districts around and produce some of the highest student success in the country, let's address how their values sustain that positive outlook against the odds. If "We are smarter than me" were a nation, these districts would be its capital. The word that best describes their work style would have to be *collaborative*.

Many people, including educators, perhaps *especially* educators, shudder at the thought of *teamwork*. We all remember being grouped together with some task to complete, and at least one person couldn't do their part, and a few more wouldn't do their part, which left one person to complete the project alone, in order to save their grade or job. The others got a free ride and learned nothing, but it looks good.

What makes the difference between loosely defined and unaccountable "group work" and "collaboration" is the level of shared accountability. The work collaboration comes from the Latin word *collaboratus,* meaning "to labor *together*" ("collaborate," 2012). Together. They do the work, together.

The secret of great leadership districts is the "we are all in this together" mentality of the organization. There are none of the tensions so commonly found between their teachers' organizations and administration or the board. They have the shared focus on student achievement. That is the yardstick by which they measure all steps. Because the associations are focused on doing what's best for students, they don't protect poor teachers; instead they work with them through a fair and just process.

Conversely, because the board and administrators are also solely focused on student success, their hiring skills eliminate much of the need to practice their firing skills. In working together to select the best teachers, there is no blame for firing a bad teacher, as both sides selected the teacher and both sides worked together to develop the teacher. Together, teachers and administration can keep their focus on instruction and student learning.

Great leadership districts distinctly work together to set their goals, while at each school, you find building personnel leaders working collaboratively, to set their goals. The superintendents provide a template, based on the needs of the district, and trust the schools' leadership to customize that to fit the schools' needs.

This trust is based in shared leadership. All individuals face the same accountability for working together, toward success for all students. They see success for all kids as the business of their business. It's simply what they do. They work together to achieve their goals, because together, every person giving their all is the only way they can meet those goals. They are *their* goals, based on *their* needs, and on *their* vision and mission.

The shared language of these learning communities creates meaningful slogans, grown from the fertile soil of their culture. They are passionate about finding a way to make all students succeed, from the depth of their research to the height of their discussions; finding a way to make that happen is what drives their common sense of *teamness*.

These districts value their teachers. They value teachers as the content specialists they are. They value their skills in peer teaching and peer learning. They value the "teachers teaching teachers" model of staff development. Teachers find multiple levels of leadership opportunities in these districts.

Regardless of whether teachers aspire to administrative positions, or prefer to remain in the classroom, these districts identify and recruit teacher-leaders and develop their leadership skills through training and opportunity. Teachers are encouraged to share their successful teaching strategies and tools, tips of implementing lesson plans, and managing student behaviors.

Because there is *no shame, no blame, and no excuses*, teachers build strong transitions between grades, both curricular and in actual performance. In helping a teacher struggling with her class this year, other teachers may literally be helping themselves out when dealing with the same students, next year. This is a win-win situation.

Again, district and school leaders put their money where their mouths are by providing open communication and support. They invest in people, not just employees and students, but in the whole school community. They believe the school exists to serve the community, not the other way around.

In all great leadership districts, you see district leadership supporting each other, employees, students, and the community through professional development, collaboration time, clearly communicating expectations to students and parents, and welcoming their communities to have input through town hall meetings, and more. No school is a world unto itself; it truly takes a village to raise a child . . . and these leaders know it, breathe it, live it.

HABITUAL VALUES REFLECTION

All people have values, things we believe, things we cherish. Not all people share the same values, even when confined to a single role in life. We differ in our "family" values, our "religious" values, and yes, even our "work" values. The leaders we have studied do share common "school" values, and that is at the core of what makes their districts so high performing. They value student success, teaching and teachers, human growth and professional development, finding a way to make everything possible, and mostly, they value human dignity.

The most simplified reason for the success of the great leadership within schools and districts lies in the value placed on teaching and learning by their leaders. Through common vision and mission, administrators and teacher associations have developed peaceful relationships, focused on the success of each student. They share accountability in teachers' ability to create that success, because they hire the teachers together, they develop the teachers together, and on the rare occasion, they fire the teachers together. The latter rarely happens in part due to the quality of their hires, plus the tremendous support provided the teachers.

New teacher induction and meaningful professional development sessions when combined with collaboration and peer support develop novice teachers *and* challenge master teachers. When students need more time to master the curriculum, school leaders arrange the resources to accommodate more time. Because all district employees value student success above all, they find ways to make students successful. This defines *who* they are and *what* they do.

No shame, no blame, no excuses. This appears to be a clarion cry of all great districts, inherent in all of them. When Johnny can't read, there is no shame. The child is not blamed, nor the parents, nor last year's teacher. It is, however, considered an unacceptable state, and it will be corrected. No excuses offered or accepted.

If the data indicates a modified school calendar is needed, to provide accelerations and extensions, district leadership finds a way to allocate resources to do so. The same principle applies to extended school days and tutoring. Data drives the decision making, and that is why everyone is trained to analyze it, discuss it, and determine how to improve it.

The value for human dignity that these employees share prevents students from becoming numbers, and teachers from being pawns. Because data drives decisions from the bottom up, recommendations are rife with the human element. That 1 percent who can't read? Some may consider that great, but with these districts, that 1 percent has names, they are someone's babies, and they matter. They will learn to read. That's what excelling districts value and what great leaders do.

CHAPTER LEARNING EXTENSIONS

Testing Your Understanding of This Chapter about Values

Look over the matrix in table 2.1 and compare your understanding to those of the authors. Remember that your response should be two-edged; that is, how it looks gazing through the lens of the chapter and then a second skeptical examination of the lens itself. Remember that knowledge is never neutral. It exists within human hierarchies of power and how one values others. One can ask, "Who benefits from this knowledge, and who doesn't?" The answer will provide clues as to the actual power relationships involved and the inherent values embedded.

Table 2.1. What Do You Believe about Values?

Statement	What do you think? True/false? Yes/no?	Where you are in your understanding
2.1. Being a school leader is the perfect opportunity to make a name for the leader.		
2.2. Valuing human dignity can ease tension between administration and associations.		
2.3. It takes a village to raise a child.		
2.4. Developing a "common language" is a fad buzzword.		
2.5. Teachers are the key to student success.		

3

THE MOST IMPORTANT KNOWLEDGE BEGINS WITH SELF

Leaders have nothing but themselves to work with.

—Warren Bennis (1989, p. 47)

Leadership knowledge is most often conceptualized as external to the leader. We think of skills and competencies or perhaps in former times traits or habits. Undeniably leadership has its skill sets. However, great leaders have to make themselves. Leadership is in the end a human construct.

The most salient part of understanding leadership is that it is co-constructed with others. And this co-construction occurs in a relationship to common challenges or tasks. The construction of leadership is essentially interactive, cultural, and contextual. What we often miss about leadership is the continuous act of co-construction. When we take our eyes away from the followers who define leadership, we only see half of leadership.

Knowledge of self does not come easy to anyone. Understanding ourselves is part and parcel of growing in consciousness and the ability to step outside ourselves and look objectively at who we are, what we want, and why we want it. Dean Acheson, U.S. secretary of state, once recalled that President Harry Truman was "free of the greatest vice in a leader, his ego never came between him and his job" (McCullough, 1992, p. 755).

This quest does not occur in a vacuum but is embedded in cultural value systems and what we should be, what we should want, and why we should want it. We learn to confront the tension between what is good for us and what is good for others and the antinomy between them. It is a lifelong challenge because the common good is not always "common."

We also learn the importance of others in our own construction of self. Great leaders were not always "great." For example, Winston Churchill was a school bully and was placed in a remedial class for "dullards" (Keegan, 2002, p. 26).

Mohandas Gandhi was afraid of the dark, stole cigarettes as a child, and was a failure as a lawyer because he was afraid of public speaking. Louis Fischer, Gandhi's biographer, says of him, "It is not that he turned failure into success. Using the clay that was there he turned himself into another person. His was a remarkable case of second birth in one lifetime" (1950, p. 40).

Dolores Huerta, the mother of the United Farm Workers Union, was accused of cheating in school because her papers were too good for a Mexican; was twice divorced; slept in her car; and was later accused of being a negligent mother by her second husband (Schiff, 2005).

Harry Truman, who commanded an artillery battery in World War I with heroic distinction, remembers that as a boy he wore glasses and was a "kind of sissy" who ran from fights. He played the piano and read books by Plutarch and Shakespeare (McCullough, 1992, p. 45). He once wrote to his daughter, "Always be nice to the people who can't talk back to you. I can't stand a man or woman who bawls out underlings to satisfy an ego" (McCullough, 1992, p. 569).

We will deal with the matter of leadership identity in chapter 5. Perhaps the most important thing to remember about the kind of knowledge most important to great leaders was spoken by Thales (635–543 BC), a Greek philosopher and scientist who said, "Know thyself" (The Quotations Page, n.d.).

THE SECOND KIND OF KNOWLEDGE: THE ANCHOR OF PROFESSIONAL PRACTICE

Great leaders have a fundamental understanding about the external knowledge involved in anchoring leadership. They understand that professional practice is anchored to a set of larger content and that what is known most likely contains much of what is not true. They understand that what we know is filled with errors, so they have developed a healthy skepticism about current professional practice.

They believe, but they also disbelieve simultaneously. While such leaders are "acting" and "doing" leadership, they are also questioning those same actions and especially the assumptions upon which they are based. They also understand that what they know that they don't know is as important as what they do know. Leaders that have no grasp of the limitations of their own knowledge are, to put it simply, dangerous.

We think here of the political leaders and generals who had no understanding of Vietnamese culture or history that won battles but lost the war in Vietnam because of a false belief in the so-called "domino theory" in which they saw the Chinese and the Vietnamese joined in force to dominate Southeast Asia (Spartacus Educational, n.d.). They *failed* to understand that the Chinese and Vietnamese were thousand-year-old enemies.

Professional practice swims within a discourse. A discourse consists of all of the beliefs, assumptions, biases, prejudices, and actions that are both written and spoken. The paradox of a discourse is that it is not itself questioned, but it is the medium through which we ask questions. In short a discourse "operates behind [our] backs, it is an unthought" (Foucault, 1974, p. 49).

Understanding the limitations of knowledge begins with observing that when it comes to professional practice, knowledge cannot be allowed to become dogma. It must be constantly scrutinized. Charles Sanders Peirce (1955) summarized this position when he said, "There are three things to which we can never hope to attain by reasoning, namely absolute certainty, absolute exactitude, absolute universality. We cannot be absolutely certain that our conclusions are even approximately true" (p. 54).

The current derivation of a "knowledge base" in educational administration falls into this same dilemma. In short, it has become our contemporary "philosopher's stone" in which in medieval times it was believed lead could be turned into gold (English, 2011).

PROFESSIONAL PRACTICE BASED ON DOGMA LEADS TO TRAGIC MISTAKES

Professional practice in any field is shot through with fallacies and falsehoods. Medical doctors have killed patients by the score because of what they believed to be true that was simply wrong. Prior to Pasteur's discovery of bacteria in wine, doctors routinely infected patients with unwashed hands, from those patients upon whom they had amputated limbs to pregnant women who were infected with "childbirth fever" by their attending physicians (Nuland, 2003) or bled other patients to death because of a false understanding of how much blood was actually in the body.

Medicine was practiced long before it became a "science" and was filled with errors even after it became *scientific*. There are in every discourse narratives which connect means and ends, stories about what causes what, and what can be changed (or "cured" or "reformed"). When these are beliefs not subjected to challenge they are called "ideologies," and some are very powerful even in the face of contrary evidence.

For example, even when it was shown that peptic ulcers were not caused by excess stomach acid but by bacteria, medical doctors refused to accept that antibiotics could "cure" such ulcers because of the overriding belief that bacteria could not live in the stomach (LeFanu, 1999). Here was a powerful ideology, one which prevented many patients from actually being cured of peptic ulcers, even when factual evidence existed challenging this dominant narrative.

Education has also had its share of ideologies. Racism and sexism in schools existed (and still exists) because it was not believed minorities could learn as well as the White majority; girls were inferior to boys in mental and physical capacities; and only the Protestant Bible could be read in the public schools because it alone was the one true way (see Tyack, 1974).

The history of medical practice also confirms how irrefutable scholars or practitioners' wisdom must similarly be scrutinized. The most famous physician of antiquity was Galen (c130–c200), who wrote sixteen books on medicine and whose influence held back the advance of medicine for centuries. Despite the fact that his works were based on empirical evidence, Galen never dissected humans, only animals. So when it came to prescriptions based on animal dissections, he got it wrong.

No one who performs research should be above question, no matter their reputation (Nuland, 2003). No one's "body of evidence" should be without review and no "knowledge" should be accepted without serious skepticism, especially if it is based on "the wisdom of the field" (Murphy, 2000). The wisdom of the field in educational leadership once advanced the idea that women could not be effective school leaders because they could not reason well and were too emotional (Blount, 1998; Brunner,

1999; Shakeshaft, 2011). In addition there was rampant homophobia (Fry-and & Capper, 2003) and overt and covert racism (Lopez, 2003).

Knowledge becomes dogma when it is not recognized that:

1. There is no epistemological ground on which the indubitable truth of knowledge statements can be established;
2. A body of knowledge consists of fragments of understanding, not a system of logically integrated statements;
3. Knowledge is a construction built out of cognitive schemes and embodied interactions with the environment; and
4. The test of a knowledge statement is its pragmatic usefulness in accomplishing a task, not its derivation from an approved set of methodological rules. (Barlosky, 2006, p. 544)

THE FALLACY OF "RESEARCH-BASED" KNOWLEDGE AS SUPERIOR

It has become trendy to talk about *researched-based knowledge* as though this sobriquet will somehow give some knowledge superiority over that which is non-research based. Unless one knows exactly what has been researched with what procedures, under what conditions, employing what assumptions and by whom, designating some knowledge as "research based" gives it no special status.

There is a whole bunch of so-called "research" being pumped out by neoliberal think tanks that has been exposed by the National Education Policy Center (NEPC) at the University of Colorado at Boulder as shoddy and ill formed without being properly vetted in peer-reviewed procedures (NEPC, 2012). Even when properly done, very few one-shot research studies are or can be definitive (English, 2007).

Anyone who has done research or supervised research understands how tenuous and fragile research activity really is. This is especially true with leadership research, where the variables are so interactive, complex, and contextually situated that most research is highly qualitative in nature from which robust generalizations are nearly impossible to formulate. Even good research in the area of leadership is mostly suggestive. It's not like finding the best way to teach reading or fractions.

The National Research Council's (2002) guidelines for conducting so-called "scientific research" doesn't work with educational leadership because randomized trial groups do not exist in school system administration. Educational leadership is more complicated and complex than even classroom applications and interactions, mostly because educational leadership is highly politicized and does not follow predetermined procedures that lend themselves to purely rational approaches.

This is one reason why there is a plethora of books regarding leadership which have come to be called "kitsch" management and offer simplified solutions and happy endings in noncomplicated settings (Papa, Kain, & Brown, in press). Beginning with Covey's (1991) best-selling book *The Seven Habits of Highly Successful People* being exposed as lacking empirical validation and consisting of an implicit sectarian-based approach disguised as scientific (English, 2002), "kitsch" books have proliferated in the marketplace, from Jim Collins's *Good to Great* to Spencer Johnson's (2002) *Who Moved My Cheese?*

Perhaps the best observation about such books was proffered by *The Economist* (2004) in an article titled "How 51 Gorillas Can Make You Seriously Rich." Of course, the most perceptive leadership literature was written 400 years ago by William Shakespeare, and some of today's most readable books discuss the techniques of past heroes, such as Alexander the Great. "They will teach you history, even if they do not make you Jack Welch" (p. 69).

We believe that research about leadership is certainly merited, but we do not agree that the former largely positivistic models will tell us much more than we already know. We agree with Heilbrunn's (1996) commentary:

> The scientific quest for a generic model of leadership can take one only so far. Employing factor analysis to quantify leadership and focusing so minutely on the qualities of leadership, the field repeatedly loses sight of one of the principal reasons for its subject's essentially unpredictable nature—the environment in which leaders function. Or, to put it another way, leadership studies lacks an adequate concern for context, historical or situational. (p. 8)

IPSA SCIENTIA POTESTAS EST: THE POLITICS OF KNOWLEDGE

Sir Francis Bacon (1561–1626) wrote that "knowledge is power" (The Quotations Page, p. 1). Indeed, knowledge is never neutral because it benefits some and works to the disadvantage of others. Power and knowledge are intimately connected (Foucault, 1980) because human society is hierarchically layered, and so information aids some within that hierarchy differentially. The same is true with the knowledge we consider here as essential to great leaders in education.

So, what is it we know of great leadership in educational settings? We understand some tenets of the continuum of poor leadership to functional leadership to great leadership. Here we proffer some examples of how one can reflect on the knowledge of leadership; that is, leadership that grows and changes based on continual knowledge gathering.

I. Current Issue Analysis: The Great Leaders Mentoring Knowledge

Mentoring instructional and administrative leadership will ensure a potent modeling of behavior within the educational organization (Wagner, 2010). Knowing how to mentor is a skill great leaders develop over time and experience. Mentoring is considered to be the highest human skill one can develop (Papa [Papalewis], 1987). Why we mentor others requires our understanding of motivation in the workplace and its importance in the organization.

The importance of helping others to continually become better at their life is a gift that all of us can develop. Many studies have been done that tell those studying leadership what we have come to learn if we pay attention to caring for one another.

- Sharing of information about the workplace
- Providing feedback
- High on-site visibility
- Effective communication
- Supporting professional development opportunities
- Developing listening skills
- Deciding on synchronous and asynchronous open door practices
- Setting goals
- Doing reality checks
- Giving emotional support
- Knowing adult learning theories and practices
- Encouraging creativity

- Organizing communities of learners
- Teaching professional behaviors
- Modeling mentoring

All of these practices and more are skills that can be developed if one has the knowledge of their value. "Effective superintendents spend significant time instructing, training, and coaching" (Wagner, 2010, p. 97). Valuing how to treat those working for you in the workplace is more important than bringing in programs, as piecemeal approaches often fall short.

Knowledge of the mentoring processes or stages of mentoring (Mullen, 2012; Papa [Papalewis], 1987) tells the ebb and flow of mentoring. Organized procedures for mentoring new teachers/faculty/workers through induction programs increases success with new employees. Knowledge of how to set up a program, knowing whom to involve as mentors, and deciding on the length of time required are all processes that require understanding.

Likewise, mentoring occurs without specific organized programs. It is human nature when human beings are working together for a common good, such as in education, that friendships form. A strong, people-focused environment builds a culture that will support mentors with no fear of being a person desiring to be a mentee. A strong culture of care and respect is found in a great leader's repertoire.

Many have written about the stages of mentoring. Briefly, these focus on the changing phases, from novice-mentor to ultimately mentor-to-mentor.

2. Current Issue Analysis: Leading Curriculum Improvement

Real knowledge of curriculum improvement requires more than what the publishing companies use in their marketing strategies to convince a purchase. The drill down of the common core standards are focused on the written or intended curriculum. Tallerico (2012), building off the writings of English (2010) and others, describes the intended curriculum as the current focus of schooling, for it focuses on what is written, taught, and tested (p. 5). So, what is not taught formally becomes the unintended curriculum.

The knowledgeable leader knows that the unintended curriculum is critical to assess and monitor. Is a liberal education considered to be still important? How and where are democratic ideals taught? Where does social justice fit in? If all we are asked to do is measure, test, and assess students, what else does the school leader need to know so as to ensure a fully enriched curriculum? As Gordon and Bridglall (2005) remind us, schools should "contribute to civic life, form and strengthen families, value and contribute to the arts, and respect local culture and traditions" (p. 59).

3. Current Issue Analysis: Student Retention in Theory and in Practice

The knowledgeable leader is the smart leader. Some issues require knowing the pro/con and not just what is currently being pushed at either the federal or state levels. One of these issues is student retention.

Retention is critical to understand. Beginning with the No Child Left Behind Act of 2001 (PL107-110, 2001), which led to today's Common Core Standards, retention assessments are expected at the end of third and eighth grade.

Arguments for Retention   Since the scathing report *A Nation at Risk* was issued during President Reagan's first four years, all subsequent federal legislation since 1983 has ratcheted up standards, proof of student proficiency, and assessments to evaluate the effectiveness of the learner and teacher. Retention of students is the current vogue: assessing students in grades three and eight by assessments and teacher review to determine retention.

There is research that may justify retention based on the social or lack of social skills the student displays: lack of grade-level maturity (Xia & Glennie, 2005) and social awkwardness (Hu, 2008). Time may benefit this student, to allow them to grow into a maturity that is not based on age but on ability to acquire skills in the time-on-task classroom.

Likewise, retention can be blamed on the student for their *poor* choices and for lack of correct family involvement. Blaming the family unit or the students themselves absolves the school, state, and federal policy makers from sharing the blame, while establishing rigorous benchmarks. Another thought is the fear that since Susie failed, it will motivate others to try harder (Thompson & Cunningham, 2000).

Arguments against Retention   Numerous research studies tell us that retention is not a good practice. Research on not retaining students presents several primary reasons:

- Retained students have significantly more behavior problems and lower peer acceptance (Frey, 2005).

- Retained students are at a higher risk of dropping out of school (Eide & Showalter, 2001).
- Students that are retained in early primary grades do worse academically than other low-performing students who were not retained (Alexander, Entwisle, & Dauber, 2003).
- Retained students report feeling shame and embarrassment (Aldridge & Goldman, 2006).
- One year retained students are five times more likely to drop out than their never-retained peers (Karweit, 1991).
- Students who have been held back twice have a 90 percent probability of dropping out of school (Silberglitt et al., 2006).

In the current educational times, assessment achievement must be proved by the school and district or federal/state funds may be withheld. This removes from the hands of the school/district leaders a more thoughtful individual approach. According to Black (2008), children understand the notion of failure as young as age three.

4. Current Issue Analysis: Technology and Its Role in Teaching and Learning/Social Media

The ubiquitous nature of technology in society and its influence on the learner does not necessarily mean all is good with it. The business approach of adapt-adopt-scale-up leads the marketing push to create online courses and products that even claim that teachers are not required, not to mention school buildings. For example, *The Common Core Standards Initiative for English Language Arts* (2011) states the following:

> To be ready for college, workforce training, and life in a technological society, students need the ability to gather, comprehend, evaluate, synthesize, and report on information and ideas, to conduct original research in order to answer questions or solve problems, and to analyze and create a high volume and extensive range of print and non-print texts in media forms old and new. The need to conduct research and to produce and consume media is embedded into every aspect of today's curriculum. In like fashion, research and media skills and understandings are embedded throughout the Standards rather than treated in a separate section. (p. 1)

The Common Core Standards Initiative for Mathematics (2011) states the following:

> Mathematically proficient students consider the available tools when solving a mathematical problem. These tools might include pencil and paper, concrete models, a ruler, a protractor, a calculator, a spreadsheet, a computer algebra system, a statistical package, or dynamic geometry software.
>
> Proficient students are sufficiently familiar with tools appropriate for their grade or course to make sound decisions about when each of these tools might be helpful, recognizing both the insight to be gained and their limitations. For example, mathematically proficient high school students analyze graphs of functions and solutions generated using a graphing calculator. They detect possible errors by strategically using estimation and other mathematical knowledge.
>
> When making mathematical models, they know that technology can enable them to visualize the results of varying assumptions, explore consequences, and compare predictions with data. Mathematically proficient students at various grade levels are able to identify relevant external mathematical resources, such as digital content located on a website, and use them to pose or solve problems. They are able to use technological tools to explore and deepen their understanding of concepts. (pp. 1–2)

As evident by these two examples, Common Core Standards technology is deeply embedded in the nationalized curriculum that will prepare U.S. students for college and/or entering the workforce. Within the English language arts Common Core Standards is the language of print or non-print materials, as is the production and consumption of media materials. If there was any doubt of the use of software media in this standard, the mathematics Common Core Standards states that use of technological tools will "deepen" the understanding of concepts.

Umpstead (2009) sums up nicely, "Online learning may also have a place in your school's summer, credit recovery, and alternative or adult education programs, helping students complete course work they either couldn't or wouldn't finish within the normal course of their education" (p. 68).

Other researchers concur. Dessoff (2009) writes, "Many [districts] are adopting online solutions offered by commercial vendors, and others are implementing programs that blend face-to-face and online instruction. Some create their own programs from free online resources and their own curricula" (p. 44). This is called credit recovery and ensures another option: greater student enrollment.

Not all agree. Darrow (2010) writes:

> In operating on that belief about comparative cost advantages, the administrators were holding to one of the biggest myths about online, or virtual, school programs. What they overlooked is this: Various costs must be factored into the development, implementation and maintenance of a strategically planned online school or virtual program for it to become financially sustainable. (p. 26)

5. Current Issue Analysis: Trends of the Day in Common Core State Standards

Common Core State Standards is the new surrogate national curriculum: a drill down of curriculum that can be assessed through the No Child Left Behind (NCLB, 2001) and Race to the Top acts (HR 6244, 2010). When President Obama (2009) spoke to the Hispanic Chamber of Commerce, he "labeled the current variability of education standards inexcusable and called on states to implement tougher, clearer standards . . . stop low-balling expectations for our kids" (p. 2).

Thus the genesis of national standards formed by the Council of Chief State School Officers and the National Governors Association developed the Common Core Standards (National Governors Association Center for Best Practices, Council of Chief State School Officers, 2010) that quickly had forty-plus states replacing their state specific standards with the Common Core Standards (Conley, 2011). Teachers, parents, and community leaders have all weighed in to help create the Common Core State Standards.

> The standards clearly communicate what is expected of students at each grade level. This will allow our teachers to be better equipped to know exactly what they need to help students learn and establish individualized benchmarks for them. The Common Core State Standards focus on core conceptual understandings and procedures starting in the early grades, thus enabling teachers to take the time needed to teach core concepts and procedures well—and to give students the opportunity to master them.
>
> With students, parents and teachers all on the same page and working together for shared goals, we can ensure that students make progress each year and graduate from school prepared to succeed in college and in a mod-

ern workforce. (National Governors Association Center for Best Practices, Council of Chief State School Officers, 2010, p. 1)

Rothman (2012) believes the Common Core Standards make clear what students need to know and do for succeeding in college and in their careers. Some believe these Common Core Standards will lead to equity for all students: all students receive the same curriculum; all are tested using the same tests; and those students that move between districts will no longer be penalized (Barton, 2010; Meier, Schmidt, Finn, Schlechty, & Zhao, 2010).

The website for the Common Core Standards states:

These standards define the knowledge and skills students should have within their K–12 education careers so that they will graduate high school able to succeed in entry-level, credit-bearing academic college courses and in workforce training programs. The standards:

- Are aligned with college and work expectations;
- Are clear, understandable and consistent;
- Include rigorous content and application of knowledge through high-order skills;
- Build upon strengths and lessons of current state standards;
- Are informed by other top performing countries, so that all students are prepared to succeed in our global economy and society; and
- Are evidence-based. (Common Core State Standards Initiative, 2011, p. 1)

The other side has some concerned with the extreme narrowing of the curriculum, that is, learning for learning's sake with no intended and obvious reason is now a concept of the past. Some believe that local control tied to responsibility has ended (Allen, 2009) and now, how will local social issues such as poverty come into play? The federal heavy-handedness has made states feel obligated to climb on board to receive federal dollars.

But even more important is that the Common Core Standards still represent Bourdieu and Passeron's (2000) *cultural arbitrary* as an elite cultural construct that is neither universal nor "common" to all groups and to all peoples, even in the same society. The adoption of only one form of curriculum is an example of symbolic power, and it enfranchises some and disenfranchises other groups. Furthermore, there is a huge economic interest in the Common Core Standards as textbook and other companies stand to gain with a host of prepackaged products ready to sell for the new market created by the new curriculum. It is a myth that any new set of standards that imposes only one type of curriculum will reduce the achievement gap when the gap is built into the system itself.

6. Current Issue Analysis: Families and Communities

The changing student faces found in our schools today are not the faces of the past. Knowledge that focuses on your family and community demographics is critical to gather and digest. Great leaders ensure that the teachers and staff are focused on social justice realities. The ever-changing demographics require a dedication to understanding poverty and its effects on student learning and family life. Knowledge on how tests are biased is part of this equation.

Power and privilege dynamics that work to keep the *poor* poor (Barry, 2005) while keeping those privileged from recognizing their privileges is what Bourdieu calls *misrecognition* (Webb, Schirato, & Danaher, 2002, p. xiv). Knowledge of the vast discrepancy between educational accountability must be analyzed through the disparities of wealth distribution across U.S. society for a robust perception of educational achievement.

CHAPTER LEARNING EXTENSIONS

Testing Your Understanding of This Chapter about Knowledge

Look over the matrix in table 3.1 and compare your understanding to those of the authors. Remember that your response should be two edged; that is, how it looks gazing through the lens of the chapter and then a second skeptical examination of the lens itself. Remember that knowledge is never neutral. It exists within human hierarchies of power. One can ask, "Who benefits from this knowledge, and who doesn't?" The answer will provide clues as to the actual power relationships involved.

Table 3.1. What Do You Believe about Knowledge?

Statement	What do you think? True/false? Yes/no?	Where you are in your understanding
3.1. Leaders are born and not made.		
3.2. Knowledge of self is a relatively easy task to do and only requires persistence.		
3.3. Dogma is present in education and in educational leadership practice.		
3.4. When some people say a practice is "research based," you should believe it is true.		
3.5. Knowledge is power.		

4

THE ACQUISITION AND REFINEMENT OF SKILLS AND INSIGHTS TO INSPIRE OTHERS

Learning on the job, day after day, is the work.

—Michael Fullan (2008, p. 86)

Context matters. To illustrate this point, picture yourself taking a walk. Your mind's eye might conjure a stroll through a residential neighborhood, a barefoot amble on a sandy beach, or a gentle descent through a forest glade. If the context were to change, with the neighborhood now changed to a scene of rioting, the beach transformed during a hurricane's landfall, and the forest's trail now angling up a 12 percent grade on an exposed ridge, the walker's knowledge of the context, along with the walker's skill in negotiating the adverse conditions, become critical factors.

Today's public school leaders face very challenging conditions. The focus of this chapter is the skills these leaders need to successfully negotiate the path that lies ahead.

For some time, the metaphor of an "uphill climb" has been used to describe the challenges faced by public schools and school leaders. Beginning in the post–World War II years, education reformers began to be harshly critical of schools for poorly preparing students to keep step with scientific and military developments in the Soviet Union. The 1957 launch of the Sputnik by the Soviet Union was a defining moment in the history of U.S. public education (NASA, 2007). The ensuing years saw an increase

mic standards in schools, with a particular focus on mathematics
nce courses.

By the mid-1950s, *Brown v. Board of Education* (n.d.), the Civil Rights
movement, and later, President Lyndon Johnson's War on Poverty shifted
attention not only to competition with the Soviet Union, but also to the just
demand for equality of opportunity in schools. Funding for education was
substantially increased in the 1970s, as ambitious federal programs were
initiated in an effort to respond to concerns for civil rights and to combat
the effects of poverty and other barriers to learning.

Frustration related to these efforts mounted in the late 1970s, however,
as a chorus of critics began to call attention to the perceived shortcomings
of these federal programs. A number of prominent critics came to blame
the schools for contributing to a poorly prepared workforce and for the
loss of market share to nations such as Japan and Germany (Cuban, 2001).

By the early 1980s, blaming public education for the nation's economic
ills became commonplace. National commission reports of the early 1980s
included the National Commission on Excellence in Education's *A Nation at Risk* (Brookings Institution, 1983) and the Twentieth Century Task
Force on Federal Educational Policy's *Making the Grade* (Petersen, 1983).

Such reports initiated the first of various waves of reform visited upon
schools. These reports, and their multifarious offspring over the last two
decades, launched demands for increased accountability and higher student achievement, and have shifted the expectation for public education in
the United States from a system of universal access to a system of universal
proficiency (Lewis, 2003).

Today's principals and superintendents function in a context shaped
by the rise of not only high stakes testing as a means of holding schools
accountable, but also one that is heavily influenced by a number of free
market accountability approaches, generally focused on competition for
students. Widespread school choice and school privatization plans have
proliferated across the states and at the federal level, reflecting a belief
that schools will improve only when market forces compel them to do so
(Leithwood & Earl, 2000).

The ongoing systemic reforms of recent decades, including standards-
based accountability, high-stakes testing, competition for students, and
greater activism by state and national policy makers, have set the stage for
the high degree of exposure and accountability that school leaders now

face. These factors have had a major influence on educational leadership, and those in leadership positions have found themselves contending with often contradictory expectations.

Within the current high-stakes context, administrators at both the school and district levels are called upon to align their practices with the measurable outcomes on which they and their schools will be judged. Leaders must assimilate understanding not only of a wide range of reporting and performance requirements associated with state and federal standards and accountability policy, but they must also acquire fluency in existing and emerging knowledge.

This fluency in emerging knowledge relates to topics such as the Common Core State Standards (2010) promulgated by the National Governors Association and the Council of Chief State School Officers, STEM (Science, Technology, Engineering, and Mathematics) initiatives, personnel policies, brain research, instructional and assessment practices, child and adolescent development, behavioral and physiological disorders, communicable diseases, risk exposure, and students' learning styles. This list is ever changing and growing.

Demands for extensive expertise on a variety of topics and a number of other variables conspire against effective instructional leadership on the part of school leaders. Principals and other administrators are commonly held responsible for the efficient management of a wide range of school and district functions. These include but are not limited to personnel administration, budget and finance matters, student safety, technology oversight, and facilities management.

Increasingly, they are called on to manage conflicts both within and external to the organization. These demands represent the interests of public schools in communications with lawmakers and policy makers; school leaders also perform civic duties on various boards and committees.

Those leaders who manage to survive or thrive through competing reforms have done so because they have acquired the skills needed to maneuver among the conflicting purposes of schooling and ongoing calls for radical reform. A primary purpose of the present work is to identify such skills and to provide support for the argument that great leaders grow into greatness, through developing and refining their values, knowledge, and skills.

Today's leaders indeed face an "uphill climb." The men and women in leadership positions in our nation's schools would, no doubt, agree that much of the work of leading schools feels like going uphill. Whether climb-ing the south Kaibab trail to the Grand Canyon's south rim, ascending a flight of stairs at the end of a long day, or leaning into the grade on any one of San Francisco's remarkably slanted streets, it is clear that going uphill can be difficult, grinding, and exhausting work.

Those aspiring to serve as a school leader or aiming to refine existing leadership skills must begin with an acknowledgment that effective lead-ership requires that success be attained every day, and that leaders must acquire and continue to refine key skills and expertise, "learning on the job, day after day" (Fullan, 2008, p. 86). Noted Warren Bennis,

> True leaders are not born, but made, and usually self-made. Leaders invent themselves. They are not, by the way, made in a single weekend seminar, as many of the leadership-theory spokesmen claim. I've come to think of that as the microwave theory: pop in Mr. or Ms. Average and out pops McLeader in sixty seconds. (1989, p. 42)

The following discussion will describe those leadership skills that are both accounted for in research (Cuban, 2001; Leithwood & Earl, 2000; Leithwood, Louis, Anderson, & Wahlstrom, 2004; Palestini, 2012; Papa & English, 2011; Petersen, 1999; Quinn, 2002) and self-reported by highly effective practitioners.

Across the United States, thousands of public school educators in varied and diverse school districts pour their hearts into the work of helping stu-dents to prepare for college, career, and life. They do so in an environment in which serious minds question whether there still exists a social contract to ensure the education of all children, and in which economic inequity has grown at unprecedented rates.

In this environment, most school districts perform reasonably well. Some school districts have distinguished themselves through their capacity to bring students of all backgrounds and abilities to relatively higher levels of performance. When leaders from such districts are invited to reflect on the skills and expertise that foster such performance, some common points emerge. This chapter will summarize the conclusions shared by leaders from these settings about the leadership skills that are linked with student success. See chapter 6 and appendices B and C.

What are the critical skills identified by school- and district-level leaders in highly effective school districts?

GREAT LEADERS PRIORITIZE TEACHING AND LEARNING

Great leaders develop expertise in curricula, assessment practices, and instructional delivery. They know good and poor instruction when they see it, and they refuse to settle, whether they are confronted with capable classroom teachers who need to refine their craft or classroom teachers who ought not to be classroom teachers. They strive to "exercise intellectual leadership not as head teachers, but as head learners" (Murphy, 2002, p. 188).

Despite their distance from the classroom, the need for developing instructional leadership skills is as important for superintendents as it is for principals. A statewide study of Arizona superintendents (Davidson, 2005) demonstrated that superintendents in higher-performing districts reported being more involved in planning for instruction and developing principals as instructional leaders.

This study also found that superintendents in 2005 reported a significantly higher level of involvement in instructional leadership tasks than had superintendents a decade earlier, reflecting the effects of state and federal accountability policy. In highly effective districts principals and central office administrators alike report that their superintendents are engaged in providing instructional leadership.

Bredeson (1996) notes, "Despite the managerial activity trap that ensnares all but the most savvy of administrators, superintendents are still looked to for leadership in curriculum and instruction" (pp. 245–246). Kowalski (1995), in elaborating on the barriers that impede many superintendents' efforts to serve in an instructional leadership capacity, observes,

> Because most superintendents are in office for such a brief time, it is virtually impossible to accurately determine the value of their contributions. They often are bombarded with emergencies and distracted from pursuing long-range goals. They learn from experience that they will be held more accountable for managing resources and settling disputes than for attempting long-term educational initiatives. (p. 64–65)

Despite the competing interests and distractions faced by superintendents, significant school improvement will not result unless there is a high level of involvement in curriculum and instruction activities on the part of the school superintendent.

Evidence presented by various researchers has demonstrated that, when school leaders are successful in building a shared vision focused on teaching and learning that includes concern for equity and a vision of high expectations for all students, this can lead to system-wide effects that are favorable to student achievement generally and to the most needy and disadvantaged of students (Koschoreck, 2001; Papa [Papalewis] & Fortune, 2002; Quinn, 2002; Scheurich & Skrla, 2003; Togneri, 2003; Wagner, 2001).

The *great* leaders found in our search spoke of the importance of developing meaningful and substantive expertise in the areas of curriculum, instruction, and assessment. For these leaders, this demands attention to:

Becoming knowledgeable about curricula. This requires sufficient familiarity with curriculum maps to be able to know what instruction should be taking place in each classroom, as well as what discussions should be occurring in grade level meetings. In these districts, this is an expectation for leaders at all levels. As one principal stated,

We have a commitment to instructional leadership. When we interview assistant principals, we ask them questions related to curriculum, instruction, and assessment—not just about how they will handle student discipline.

Taking responsibility for ensuring articulation and continuity within and between grades. For district-level leaders, this means ensuring consistency in curricula across the district. When teachers at the same grade level provide consistent and viable curricula within the school and across the district, this provides students—particularly the most mobile and disadvantaged students—with, in the words of leaders in one district, an *insurance policy* that reduces the likelihood that learning gaps will develop.

This also helps to provide support to teachers who are new to the grade level or the profession, since other teachers can provide vitally important information about instructional strategies or resources related to upcoming content or skills. A principal in one of the exemplary districts noted, *The content has changed, but we have had a common curriculum in place for over 30 years. This gives teachers common ground for conversations.*

The notion of a guaranteed, viable curriculum being provided to all students is deemed as essential in these school districts. Within these districts, abdicating the responsibility for closely aligning classroom practices with intended learning outcomes would be unacceptable, as this would leave important decisions about learning to the whims of individuals.

Developing a common vocabulary. A common language used by teachers, academic coaches, and administrators helps to ingrain critical components of the instructional delivery model in the school and district. A common vocabulary helps to express the organization's cultural norms and to articulate what is important in the lifeblood of the school and district.

Great leaders report that there is a common language used by academic coaches, administrators, teachers, and support staff. In these districts, terms such as "collaboration," "reteach," "intervention," "enrichment," "spiraling," "continuous improvement," "modeling," "learning system," "retraining," and "instructional model" have weight and meaning for those within the district.

Great leaders from each district state that familiarity with the district's common vocabulary begins during new teacher induction. Leaders report that *A common language is introduced at induction. It's reinforced in the mentoring program and in the evaluation system.*

Prioritizing learning for everyone in the organization. Leaders in these exemplary districts gave examples of multiple approaches to supporting the professional development of staff, including new teacher induction, mentoring, learning from peers, district-sponsored workshops, coaching, and participation in state and national conferences. One spoke with evident pride of the high expectations for teachers: *We want teachers to teach like champions.*

Ensuring that learning objectives are posted and students know where they are and what they mean. Leaders spoke of the importance of creating a classroom culture in which there are high expectations and in which students know what is expected of them.

Monitoring instruction to be certain that it is tailored and differentiated to individual students' needs. This requires that both principals and central office administrators consistently observe and discuss classroom instruction. Individuals in these districts spoke of the importance of using data on individual students to inform and guide instruction, and not simply looking at aggregated data by classroom or grade level.

They also spoke of the importance of ensuring that teachers at the same grade level or in the same discipline administer curriculum-based assessments in a consistent manner and at the same time, in order to facilitate dialogue related to teaching strategies and students' instructional needs. Notes Michael Fullan, "When data are precise, presented in a nonjudgmental way, considered by peers, and used for improvement as well as for external accountability, they serve to balance pressure and support" (2008, p. 98).

Guaranteeing that each child has a capable teacher. For these great leaders, fulfilling this guarantee involves providing adequate compensation to attract and retain qualified teachers, supporting them by providing them with instructional resources and training, and being willing to "weed the garden" of teachers who fail to meet students' needs. It also means being honest with teacher candidates about the district's expectations: *We tell candidates, if you don't like what you're hearing, then this is probably not the place for you.*

GREAT LEADERS BUILD STRONG CONNECTIONS

Larry Cuban has pointed out that no superintendent can "secretly improve a school district" (1984, p. 147). The work of school leaders is done through and with others, and great leaders pay attention to the qualities that build trust, respect, and commitment in those around them. They guide the establishment of a shared vision, they mentor, they collaborate well with colleagues at other levels and in other locations inside and outside the organization, and they make a habit of expressing loyalty, both to the organization and to their colleagues within the organization.

Building strong connections also involves creating a strong sense of purpose in the people within the organization. Fullan notes, "When peers interact with purpose, they provide their own built-in accountability, which does not require close monitoring but does benefit from the participation of the leader" (2008, p. 32). Great leaders foster commitment to the shared vision and help people to feel that the work being done matters. Such connections are what Bolman and Deal had in mind in saying of a leader, "For people to feel significant, he knew the organization had to be *ours*, not *mine*" (2001, p. 103).

The leaders of exemplary districts provided many examples of the ways in which connections are strengthened. For these leaders, this involves:

Leading by doing. In each district, great leaders spoke of the importance of setting an example for others, of walking the talk. Leading by doing requires that leaders hold high expectations not only for others, but for themselves first and foremost. If leaders expect others to admit errors, then leaders must admit errors. If leaders expect staff to be respectful toward students, then leaders must model respect toward students. As one leader said, *If we expect teachers to collaborate and share ideas, then we have a responsibility to do this as well.*

Said another, *Integrity is modeled from the top down.* Great leaders recognize that strong connections are built on trust, and that in order to have trusting, mutually supportive relationships, they must be models of ethical and professional behavior.

Growing leadership at all levels of the organization. In high-performing districts, leaders commit to mentoring others and to growing leadership from within the organization. One superintendent spoke of the importance of identifying prospective leaders from within the teaching ranks who demonstrate not only strong instructional knowledge and skills, but who also value and have a flair for creative problem solving. In another exemplary district, members of the administrative team speak with pride of the fact that, through the district's century-long existence, a superintendent had never been employed from outside the district.

This tradition of growing leaders from within, they note, creates a strong sense of connection among those in the organization, knowing that the talent and knowledge of members of the team are valued and respected. In this same district, the superintendent meets with all of the assistant principals each fall, posing the questions, *What are you doing to build your reputation as an instructional leader? What are you doing to contribute to student achievement?*

These two questions say a great deal about the district's commitment to the ongoing development of leaders, to recognizing assistant principals as more than simply disciplinarians, and to proactively implementing a plan of succession.

Sharing ideas, resources, and solutions. In high-performing districts, principals model collaboration, not by hoarding and hiding effective strategies and materials, but by going out of their way to make them available to colleagues in other buildings. They also encourage teachers to do the same, and they expect that other teachers and principals elsewhere in the organization will return the favor. One team member, suggesting that those in the organization have learned of the benefits of a sense of community throughout the district, noted, *It used to be more competitive; now our focus is on collaboration.*

Leaders in high-performing districts demonstrate a willingness to "take the walls down" and have conversations between schools about what is working. Said one principal, *We can take ideas, tweak them, and make them work for us in our setting and with our students.* Another noted, *We use part of the time in principal meetings to share ideas, learn, and support one another.* A principal in another district, describing a crisis at one school, said, *Everyone in this room would drop everything if one administrator needed help. I have personally experienced it when the cavalry comes.*

In contrast, it is not hard to picture the isolation and frustration of a principal left to deal with a major personal or professional crisis alone. In order to lead effectively, those in leadership positions must "learn to lead not from the apex of the organizational pyramid but from a web of interpersonal relationships—with people rather than through them" (Murphy, 2002, p. 188).

GREAT LEADERS MAINTAIN A DISCIPLINED FOCUS

Great leaders have a clear sense of purpose, they align their own actions and those of others with the organization's mission and goals, and they do not permit themselves to become distracted by either the current crisis or the next passing fad. Great leaders are also proficient at pulling out the weeds—the organizational glitches and barriers to growth—that can be resolved with systemic solutions.

This commitment to a clear purpose has emerged as an important factor in previous research on high-performing districts. Using a framework of six major functions, researchers (Murphy & Hallinger, 1986; Murphy & Hallinger, 1988) examined the instructional leadership role of superintendents in twelve effective school districts in California. Similar to the districts examined in the present study, these were districts with higher-than-expected achievement based upon students' socioeconomic background. Among the leadership practices that emerged as significant, three relate (Murphy & Hallinger, 1988) to the skill of maintaining a disciplined focus:

- *Setting goals and establishing expectations and standards.* Goals in these districts tended to focus on curriculum and instruction, and there was a strong belief that the district goals and the behavior of its leaders could influence district and school activities.

- *Establishing an instructional and curricular focus.* These districts had both a greater degree of attention to instructional and curricular activities and a greater degree of superintendent involvement in these activities.
- *Ensuring consistency in technical core operations.* Internal consistency in the areas of curriculum and instruction was prevalent in these districts, and leaders saw themselves as key agents for maintaining this consistency.

Leaders in high-performing districts provided specific examples of ways in which a disciplined focus is maintained. For these leaders, this requires:

Focusing on what to start doing, what to keep doing, and what to stop doing. High-performing districts establish clear priorities, they limit the number of priorities taken on at any one time to ensure effective implementation, and they pay close attention to progress and results. As one principal noted, *I want you to know how focused this district is. We don't chase everything, but instead focus on those things that make the biggest difference for students.*

Another district had learned from an earlier attempt at reform that produced a cumbersome and flawed plan with seventeen strategies and forty-two action plans, all of which were to be implemented simultaneously; in contrast, the district's next efforts at reform were focused, limited in scope, and produced significant achievement gains.

Committing to continuous improvement. Leaders in exemplary districts acknowledge the organization's capacity to improve and continually strive to improve the processes and outcomes for students. Although such leaders make a point of celebrating achievements, they are not satisfied that the present level of performance is the best that can be achieved. One principal noted, *As a long-term person here, this is not a district that accepts failure. We ask ourselves, What have we done so far, and what can we do to change outcomes, then we go for it.*

Moreover, such leaders recognize that, in public education, the landscape is constantly shifting. Educators are accustomed to experiencing continual changes in standards, curricula, assessments, rules for teacher certification, state and federal reporting requirements, and, importantly, public attitudes toward schools.

Leaders in high-performing districts acknowledge the constancy of change, and they recognize that what is good enough for today will not be good enough for tomorrow. As one leader said, *I realized early on in this district that they are committed to continuous improvement. It is deeply ingrained in the district that we can never be fully satisfied with where we are.* A leader from another district stated, *Our work is never done. We are constantly looking toward the next thing that we need to do.* Yet another said, *We don't settle. We recognize that we are not perfect.*

Formulating specific plans, with contingency and backup plans. Effective leaders recognize that a disciplined focus requires more than simply hiring the right people and hoping that things turn out well. Elaborating on Collins's (2001) metaphor, getting the right people on the bus and in the right seats is important, but the destination will not be reached if the bus is not in good working order, properly fueled, and headed in the right direction.

Great leadership districts do not leave curricular decisions to chance. Instead, they engage teachers and curriculum specialists in developing detailed curriculum maps in each subject; they align resources to the maps; they embed formative and summative assessments in the academic calendar; they train teachers in the use of the maps; they schedule specific time for student remediation, enrichment, and intervention; they communicate those expectations that are nonnegotiable; and they establish a framework for enabling administrators to regularly conduct walk-through observations to monitor instruction.

As one of the leaders in the study said, *Rather than waiting to see what will happen, we're preparing.* Another said, *We don't toot our own horn a lot. We're busy trying to do the right thing.*

GREAT LEADERS LEARN TO MANAGE EFFICIENTLY IN ORDER TO LEAD EFFECTIVELY

While influenced by variables such as the political, social, and cultural contexts in which they work, school leaders must find an effective balance between their political, managerial, and instructional roles. The current context of school accountability demands significant and measurable instructional improvements, yet school and district leaders cannot ignore the political and managerial dimensions of their work. To be effective leaders, they still must adequately attend to functions in areas such as personnel, school safety, budgeting, facility and grounds maintenance, transportation, food services, and parent relations.

In the words of a thirteen-year veteran superintendent of a large urban school district, "Your leadership isn't worth much of anything if you can't make the trains run on time" (Buchanan, 2004, p. 1). Initiating a dialogue involving various stakeholders about a shared vision of academic excellence will not go terribly far if the schools are perceived as poorly staffed, disorganized, overcrowded, lacking in basic supplies, or dirty.

Great leaders speak of developing specific skills to enable them to work more efficiently in order to successfully lead their schools and districts. For these leaders, developing these skills involves:

Separating leadership time and management time. Leaders identified specific ways in which they created time for attending to the responsibilities of maintaining and operating a school, while still carving out critical time for monitoring and shaping actions aligned with the school or district mission. In some cases, superintendents set the expectation that, for two full days each week, principals are to be out of their offices and in classrooms, observing instruction, interacting with teachers and students, and providing feedback related to teaching and learning.

For central office administrators in these districts, the expectation is established that they will observe in classrooms at least one day each week. During these "blackout days," it is understood that administrators will not have scheduled meetings, they will not complete clerical tasks, and they will be unavailable by telephone or e-mail, except for emergencies. This practice still leaves adequate time for managerial duties, yet communicates an important statement to those within the organization.

In the words of one leader, *The vital work of a school or district does not take place in an administrator's office—it takes place in classrooms.* Although creating and sticking with a schedule for observing instruction is difficult, for high-performing districts, this is a critical role for administrators. In the words of one leader, just as is the case with other resources such as funding, instructional materials, and talent, *Where organizations place their resources tells what's important to the organization. Student achievement is important, so our time and money is devoted to student achievement.*

Creating specific processes for routine tasks. Just as teachers in highly effective districts are expected to efficiently manage their classrooms by defining clear routines and procedures for students, administrators work with clerical and support staff to plan, create, and systematize procedures for addressing foreseen and unexpected needs. In some cases, administrators described regular, brief meetings with support staff to efficiently manage written and telephone communication or to process requests from staff or the central office.

This approach involves a willingness to tap into the contributions that each individual employee can offer, so that administrators can devote their time and energy to the critical work of the school. Principals also speak to the importance of collaborating with their colleagues in other settings, not just in matters involving instruction, but also to learn ways to be more efficient. Commented one, *Principals in our district are always willing to come to another school to help out.*

Using technology to expand the notion of an "open door." Access to and effective use of tools for communication were articulated by great leaders as critically important. While it is vital for leaders to develop the skill to capably use e-mail and texting to communicate with both internal and external customers, leaders noted that the importance of a commitment to responding promptly cannot be overemphasized.

In high-performing districts, there is a belief that actions speak louder than words, and that a request from a staff member or parent that is ignored or put off sends the wrong message about what the organization values. Developing the expertise and the habit of effectively using electronic communication, in these districts, opens the door to increased and improved communication.

The failure to refine one's expertise or habits in this area is viewed as either a missed opportunity, discourtesy, or mediocre leadership. In highly effective districts, there is also an acknowledgment that the use of electronic communication expands the open door, but it also expands the workday and the workweek.

The focus of this chapter is primarily on developing the skills of leadership, not the values associated with effective leadership (as noted in chapter 2). There is, however, in high-performing districts, a significant linkage between valuing collegial relationships and work ethic, and becoming skilled in the use of contemporary tools of communication.

The words of the leader from one district was representative: *Some of us work too long, but it's because we want to do it. Our superintendent sets the pace. If the superintendent is e-mailing at 10:30 at night or 3:30 in the morning, that says a lot about commitment and work ethic, and we know that's the pace we have to keep as well.*

GREAT LEADERS CHOOSE TO BE OPTIMISTS

The attitudes of leaders in high-performing schools and districts reflect optimism. In the diverse, and, at times, daunting settings in which they work, common among these leaders is a confidence that the organization and those within it will continue to improve. To create a better future for their organizations and their students, these school leaders are engaged in consciously picturing, choosing, and creating a better future.

Such a viewpoint reflects Bandura's social cognitive theory, in which he posits that one's belief in his or her ability to accomplish a specific task affects both personal and collective efficacy (Bandura, 2001). Such leadership contributes to what Hoy describes as "mindful and enabling school structures" (2003, p. 99), in which "school leaders know better than most that they must develop a capacity to detect and bounce back from mistakes" (p. 98).

A feature common to leaders in high-performing settings is their development of the skill of resiliency of spirit. For these leaders, this involves:

Embracing the role of cheerleader for the entire organization. Leaders in these districts spoke of the importance of being a champion for not only their own school, but for every school in the organization. Cheering and supporting those within one's own school, and particularly those in the most challenging settings, requires the development of self-discipline and humility.

One leader remarked, *We're proud of our whole family and that we're part of something bigger than ourselves.* Another leader alluded to the importance of *Being not just highly skilled, but passionate.* Leaders' actions must reflect a drive to excel, a commitment to give credit to others, and, in the words of one, a willingness to *Leave my troubles in the office and be positive when I'm out on campus.* As one superintendent in the study stated, *The nature of our work requires that we make a conscious effort to be mentally and emotionally ready for each new day.*

Maintaining a disciplined optimism about the organization's capacity to improve. The careers of some educators follow a too-familiar trajectory: initial idealism and optimism, followed by setback, followed by dispiritedness, followed by a jaded attitude toward the notion of progress, and ending in burnout and the death of hope. Leaders in high-performing districts report on the need to develop a resiliency to setbacks and impediments.

To some extent, organizational resiliency is, according to one principal, created during hiring decisions: *The most important thing we do is choosing who we invite to a school.* Whether adversity comes to individuals alone or the organization as a whole, adversity will come.

Great leaders speak of cultivating an attitude of determined resiliency, with continued pursuit of the organization's goals, even when a staff uprising or an unforeseen obstacle confronts the leader. Maintaining optimism cannot, however, amount to little more than cheerily ignoring dissent, or discarding the reliability and integrity upon which staff members count during a personal crisis.

Leaders in high-performing districts speak of the need for compassion, a commitment to understanding others, the demonstration of genuine empathy, and learning from, but not being overwhelmed by challenges. Effective leaders embrace dissent and diversity of opinion, knowing that an appreciation of dissent can lead to creative solutions to the problems schools face. Like the leaders Bennis describes, the leaders in the study sample "not only believe in the necessity of mistakes, they see them as virtually synonymous with growth and progress" (1989, pp. 95–96).

Optimism about the organization's capacity to improve is also manifested in a commitment to continue reading, learning, and exploring solutions. This commitment reflects both a degree of humility that there is so much more to know, and a faith that increased knowledge will ultimately yield organizational improvement. A relatively new leader, seeing the district with fresh eyes, stated, *I recently came to the district, and was impressed at the level of thinking, the professional knowledge, and the literature [to] read.*

Aside from modeling a commitment to continue learning, seeing oneself as a scholar-practitioner also reflects an attitude of optimism that the organization can be better tomorrow than it is today. This is great leadership in action.

This chapter began with an invitation to the reader to picture taking a walk. Although a solitary walk may have been imagined, if there is a single important lesson learned from considering the skills of leaders in effective organizations, it would be the lesson that effective leaders do not walk in isolation. Learning to lead more effectively requires a commitment to building relationships not just with those with whom one works on a daily basis, but with those outside the organization with the capacity to serve as models and mentors.

Leaders in our public schools face an uphill climb. Yet, by learning from the lessons of leaders in highly effective school districts, the skills of leadership can be acquired and refined. Such skills are not gained in a weekend seminar or a summer retreat, but must be developed day by day, year by year. The development of these skills may not make the climb any easier, but they hold the key to getting to the top of the hill. "People have built quite successful careers—describing the hill, measuring the hill, walking around the hill, taking pictures of the hill, and so forth. Sooner or later, somebody needs to actually climb the hill (Pfeffer, 2007, p. 137).

Good luck on your climb.

CHAPTER LEARNING EXTENSIONS

Testing Your Understanding of This Chapter about Skills

Look over the matrix in table 4.1 and compare your understanding to those of the authors. Remember that your response should be two edged; that is, how it looks gazing through the lens of the chapter and then a second skeptical examination of the lens itself. Remember that skills should be knowledge and values based. One can ask, "How are these skills developed?" The answer will provide clues as to the actual connections one has among one's values, knowledge, and skills involved.

Table 4.1.   What Do You Believe about Skills?

Statement	What do you think? True/false? Yes/no?	Where you are in your understanding
4.1. Teaching and learning must be the highest priorities of school leaders.	True	
4.2. Great leaders build strong connections.	True	
4.3. Great leaders maintain a disciplined focus.	Maybe	
4.4. Great leaders learn to manage efficiently, in order to lead effectively.	True	
4.5. Great leaders choose to be optimists.	Maybe	

5

LEADERSHIP IDENTITY, PRACTICE, AND WISDOM

It's a terrible thing to look over your shoulder when you are trying to lead and find no one there.

—Franklin Roosevelt in 1938 Chicago (Peters, 2005, p. 17)

The world *leader* from *lead* harkens back to the old English, *lithan*, "to go" or the German *leiten*, "to lead." The Latin word *duco* and such forms as *abducere* and *deducere* mean, "to lead, conduct, draw, or bring forward" in any direction as it relates to a person's opinions (Freund & Andrews, 1854, pp. 505–506).

The derivation and use of the notion of "leadership" does not say much about how one sees its development or successful use, especially in schools. Rost (1991) found no definitions of school leadership in books before 1900 (p. 47), though the notion of school management had appeared in educational texts, at least before 1850, notably in the Potter & Emerson book of 1842. This historical information indicates that the idea that those who manage schools should be seen as leaders is only a scant 112 years old.

Our view of leadership is that it is a *relational* phenomenon. Without followers leadership cannot materialize. Followers need the leaders they want to create social cohesion and bind them together in a common cause. Leaders understand this symbiotic bond, if not consciously, then almost always intuitively.

ave the threads together that build on the feel-
of followers. We have called this process of so-
ving *accoutering* (Papa & English, 2011, p. 87).
sess linguistic talent. They have to use the stories
d (Gardner, 1995). They have to verbalize the most
ers know, sometimes reaching into their psyches to
of consciousness (Lumby & English, 2009).

leaders *accouter* using the full range of human
emotions: hope, love, pride, greed, compassion, hatred, revenge, pa-
triotism, faith, shame, prejudice, and altruism. Let us look momentarily at
great leaders in history for some examples of *accoutering* before shifting
to educational leaders.

AN HISTORIC EXAMPLE OF AN *ACCOUTREMENT* FOR ALL TIME: JEANNE D'ARC

The life of Jeanne d'Arc was a mere nineteen years (1412–1431), the
period of her leadership a mere three years. But in that time she recast
and reconstituted the soul of a nation to evict its invaders and unite itself
physically. The best-selling historian Barbara Tuchman (1979) wrote of La
Pucelle d'Orleans—the Maid of Orleans:

> The phenomenon of Jeanne d'Arc—the voices from God who told her she
> must expel the English and have the Dauphin crowned King, the quality that
> dominated those who would have normally despised her, the strength that
> raised the siege of Orleans and carried the Dauphin to Reims—belongs to
> no category. (p. 588)

No great leader ever contradicted the personal characteristics of leaders more than Jeanne d'Arc. An adolescent female from common, peasant
heritage, swarthy, short, and stocky and not even passably pretty (Sackville-
West, 1936), she was unschooled, dressed as a man, wept easily for friend
and foe, wore armor for days without taking it off, even sleeping in it; she
rode over 3,000 miles on horseback when, in the beginning, she did not
know how to ride at all.

Jeanne never held command rank. Yet she made her generals stop
swearing and forbade the usual camp women from following the army.

When the time came for the attack, she insisted on no ruse tactics, but a straightforward assault on the strongest English citadel in the area. She was always more than a military leader. She had become a spiritual leader in a nation thirsting to retrieve its national soul and pride.

Jeanne d'Arc galvanized her followers' needs around her moral virtues: an approach to leadership that was described as early as Plutarch, when he wrote, "Moral good has the power to attract towards itself" (Scott-Kilvert, 1960, p. 171). Victoria Sackville-West (1936), one of her early biographers, wrote of her:

> She did possess the power to accomplish what she had undertaken. Her courage and conviction were superhuman. They were of the quality which admits no doubt and recognizes no obstacle. Her own absolute faith was the secret of her strength (p. 356).

THE AMERICAN JEANNE D'ARC: ROSA PARKS

An example of an American Jeanne d'Arc is a diminutive woman whose single act of defiance sparked the modern Civil Rights movement in December of 1955, and it brought down a monument mightier than the citadel at Orleans in the name of Jim Crow. When Rosa Parks refused to give her bus seat up to a white man in Montgomery, Alabama, and was later arrested, it set off a spark which still is being felt today. Rosa Parks was not a firebrand or an activist. She later confessed that "I was not tired physically, or no more tired than I usually was at the end of a working day. I was not old . . . I was only 42. No, the only tired I was, was tired of giving in" (Chappell, 2006, p.130).

Three hundred eighty-one days later after a bus boycott by the entire Black community, segregation was ended on buses, and the ripple effect reverberated through all aspects of American life, school, community, transportation, and housing with the banishment of legal racial segregation. Rosa Parks became a leader because followers were everywhere. They needed someone who would take that initial step and give them courage.

The understanding of the dynamics between how leaders create binding forms and ties with followers so that actions follow is deeply rooted in leader self-knowledge and identity development. To know others leaders have to begin with themselves, for as Warren Bennis (1989) observed,

"Leaders have nothing but themselves to work with" (p. 47). Coming to know oneself is not an easy prospect for anyone. Gardner (1968) once observed, "More often than not we don't want to know ourselves, don't want to depend on ourselves, don't want to live with ourselves. By middle life most of us are accomplished fugitives from ourselves" (p. 13).

A striking example of Gardner's observation is that of former heavyweight boxing champion of the world, Floyd Patterson. Patterson was one of eleven children who grew up in Bedford-Stuyvesant, one of the toughest neighborhoods of New York City. Sent to reform school for repeated juvenile offenses, he found his calling in boxing. At age seventeen he won the middleweight gold medal at the 1952 Helsinki Olympics. At age twenty-one he became the youngest heavyweight boxing champion of the world by knocking out Archie Moore.

But Floyd Patterson faced other demons. He once told a reporter:

> I think that within me, within every human being there is a certain weakness. It is a weakness that exposes itself more when you're alone. And I have figured out that part of the reason I do the things I do, and cannot seem to conquer that one world—*myself*—is because . . . is because . . . I am a coward. (Stratton, 2012, p. C5)

When a former superintendent was asked by a researcher what advice she would give to an aspiring school superintendent, she remarked, "I would say know who you are, know yourself, because you will be challenged every single day. Know what you stand for because that will be challenged every day, too" (Wheeler, 2012, p. 127). Another vivid example of a leader who transformed himself was that of Nelson Mandela, the first elected president of South Africa when all citizens could actually vote in that country.

FROM AN ANGRY YOUNG MAN TO A PERSON OF UBUNTU: AN EXAMPLE OF SELF-TRANSFORMATION

When Nelson Mandela was sentenced to life in prison at Robben Island, the South African version of the U.S. Alcatraz in San Francisco Bay, he was an "impulsive, quick-tempered activist" (Battersby, 2009, p.7). There, in a small cell, Mandela spent several decades of his life, a period of time which robbed him of precious time with his family and his wife, and his most productive years as a man. It was a time when he was stripped of his dignity and his humanity. Every effort was made to break him.

But, slowly he rebuilt himself with time to reflect and think. We think here of the comment by U.S. admiral James Stockdale, who said, "The test of character is not 'hanging in' when you expect light at the end of the tunnel, but performance of duty and persistence of example when you know no light is coming" (Ammer, 2012, p. 17).

Mandela was moved by reading the biographies of other leaders, and he learned again the African concept of *ubuntu*, which was described by Archbishop Desmond Tutu:

> A person with *Ubuntu* is open and available to others, affirming of others, does not feel threatened that others are able and good, for he or she has a proper self-assurance that comes from knowing that he or she belongs in a greater whole and is diminished when others are humiliated or diminished, when others are tortured or oppressed. (Battersby, 2009, p. 6)

As part of *ubuntu* Mandela came to a new appreciation of the common human being, one who perseveres day in and day out. And he had to learn to ignore his anger, because if he could not, it would have destroyed him. In this long, simmering, day-in-and-day-out imprisonment when it was only himself in the cell, Mandela went through a profound transformation. He remade himself under the most desperate circumstances and later recalled, "Prison not only robs you of your freedom, it attempts to take away your identity" (Battersby, 2009, p. 78).

THE MULTIFACETED NATURE OF HUMAN IDENTITY

While human beings are born into a culture, they do not enter the world with an identity. Human identity is socially constructed. It is interactive and fluid. The early years for humans are critical. James Barber (1985), who has studied the behavior and performance of U.S. presidents, indicates that the internal variables of a human being are (a) world view, (b) character, and (c) style.

A person's *world view* is how a human perceives his or her environment and "particularly [his] conceptions of social causality, human nature, and the central moral conflicts of the time" (Barber, 1985, p. 5). *Character* is a "person's stance as he confronts experience" (p. 5). *Style* is how a leader acts upon his/her *world view*.

And, to indicate how fluid the matter of identity is, Barber tells us that "character has its main development in childhood, world view in adolescence, style in early adulthood" (p. 7). So Barber's notion shows one dimension of identity as distinctly developmental in nature. This idea was supported by Maalouf (2000), who remarked, "Identity isn't given once and for all: it is built up and changes through a person's lifetime" (p. 20).

Another facet of the development of identity indicates that there are multiple identities, both below and above consciousness. The fact that there may be multiple identities below consciousness is not new nor particularly threatening. The position that there are multiple identities above consciousness is a challenging one because Western ideology posits that there can be but one identity. What else would it mean if we say "Know thyselves" instead of "Know thyself"?

The common notion of self, that is, identity, is singular and that whatever it is should be highly congruent with one's external presence or "face." Yet, as Bauman (2004) notes,

> In our fluid world, committing oneself to a single identity for life, or even for less than a whole life but for a very long time to come, is a risky business. Identities are for wearing and showing, not for storing and keeping. (p. 89)

Perhaps one of the most flagrant examples of a famous American who portrayed multiple selves was the great architect Frank Lloyd Wright. His biographer, Brendan Gill (1987), wrote of him:

> Behind a succession of masks incessantly put on and taken off, Wright achieved his unit of person and purpose not in the traditional way, by withdrawal from the world and a disciplined suppression of individual identity, but, on the contrary, by a flagrant exploitation of his identity, carried out upon the most prominent platforms available to him. (p. 501)

In fact, Holland and Lave (2001) have postulated that in the creation of a person's identity there is the momentary position of "the always-engaged-in-practice, always engaged-in-dialogue, unfinished character of history in a person" (p. 18). With this in mind the idea that one single self, eternal and unchanging, acts the same in every context and that this is the mea-

sure of credibility and authenticity is outdated, es]
conceived as a form of public theater (English, 200
Bottery (2004) said it best when he observed, "I1
creasingly defined by a set of nested identities, rath(
hegemonic national ones" (p. 143). Finally, as it pert
ers, Ackerman and Maslin-Ostrowski (2002) obser
on educational leaders who were psychologically wc

> Most school leaders, including those we interviewed, would admit that the
> role itself requires a certain amount of method acting, a style obliging a per-
> former (leader) to respond as much to his own inner feelings as the require-
> ments of the role. (p. 9)

We believe that a model of educational leadership is required that has
one leg in science and the other in art. In fact, unless leadership involves
the arts and the use of narrative, drama, and morality, effective leadership is impossible, though simplistic forms of bureaucratic managerialism
can be present. One experienced North Carolina urban superintendent
summed it up as follows:

> Really good school boards look for people who have a track record of ex-
> cellent leadership in schools or in school systems, who have demonstrated
> knowledge and focus on students and their ability to improve student
> achievement. They are looking for people who approach leadership from
> being a team as opposed to being the dictator of the school system. So you
> are looking for somebody that has the ability to collaborate, learn from oth-
> ers, but most of all inspire leadership. So they are looking for people that
> demonstrate the ability to inspire people to follow. So at the end of the day,
> that is what leadership is. (Wheeler, 2012, pp. 132–133)

CONTEXTUAL CHALLENGES: HOW THE MODEL OF *ACCOUTREMENTS* WORKS

The model of leadership which we believe is most appropriate and inclusive
of a perspective combining the science and art of leading is that of considering it as an *accoutrement*. An accoutrement comes from the Middle French
around 1596 and can be tracked to the Renaissance Latin word "accostu-
rare," which meant to arrange or to sew something (Barnhart, 1995, p. 6).

...gly we proffer that leadership is an act of sewing together ...ntity or identities into the fabric of one's culture, modes of ...unication, relationships to groups, and current mythologies and ...form of ritualized performance, that is, a form of theater (Ehrich & English, 2012; Lumby & English, 2009). That same North Carolina urban superintendent reinforced the notion that leadership is a form of public theater when she remarked:

> The superintendent's role is everything, which is what makes it such fun and such a challenge at the same time. Your role in terms of just literally, is to carry out policy. But it goes so far beyond that. You are *the face of the district* [italics the authors]. You are the spokesperson for your staff. You are the person your staff looks to you for leadership and inspiration. So it's a hugely important and complex job. (Wheeler, 2012, pp. 145–146)

The strength of the idea of leadership as an *accoutrement* is that it can take advantage of the full spectrum of human emotion and it can be centered in the notion of morality, which is of critical importance in making *social justice* an important part of the leadership of public education. Figure 5.1 displays this concept (English, Papa, Mullen, & Creighton, 2012, p. 73).

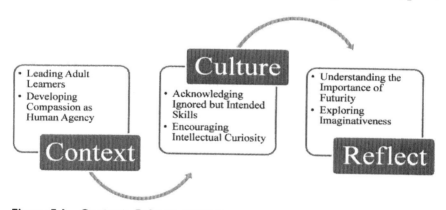

Figure 5.1. Context, Culture, Reflect

Leadership skills advance in a complex interaction of context, culture, and reflection. We see it as a continuous process with the usual spurts of growth followed by periods of relative stasis. There are two aspects to culture. The first is the culture in which the school or an educational institution is embedded. Hall (1959) defines culture as "the mold in which we are all cast, and it controls our daily lives in many unsuspected ways" (p. 38). Then in a prescient passage Hall (1959) goes on to say:

> Culture hides much more than it reveals, and strangely enough what it hides, it hides most effectively from its own participants. Years of study have convinced me that the real job is not to understand foreign culture but to understand our own. (p. 39)

Bourdieu (1984) commented,

> There is no way out of the game of culture, and one's only chance of objectifying the true nature of the game is to objectify as fully as possible the very operations which one is obliged to use in order to achieve that objectification. (p. 12)

Bourdieu & Passeron (2000) saw that schools implemented the culture of the dominant elites in the larger society. This was the "cultural arbitrary" (p. 16). The second aspect of culture is school culture, which is to a large extent a subset of the values of the dominant elites. School culture includes the "norms, values and beliefs at work in a school as well as its symbols and artifacts, the stories and myths surrounding the institution, and lastly the dominant rituals and ceremonies" (Peterson & Cosner, 2006, p. 250). We look now at the context of educational leadership as the fulcrum within which *accoutering* is interactive with culture.

CONTEXTUAL CHALLENGES TO EDUCATIONAL LEADERSHIP

The context of challenges to educational leadership has shifted over the past decades. While there have been some constants such as difficulty in securing financial resources, the increasing legislative mandates for making education better via testing and connecting test scores to administrative performance and tenure, teacher merit pay, and increased use of privatization and charter schools, have served to reduce the number of candidates actually interested in becoming educational leaders (Nussbaum, 2007). And no one disagrees that persons functioning as educational leaders today are facing increased job-related stress (Palestini, 2012).

Wheeler (2012, pp. 70–71) analyzed factors which led to superintendent turnover in North Carolina. Wheeler's research was a mixed method study of a sample of the 115 school superintendents in the state regarding factors which led to turnover, and interviews of eight retired or semiretired superintendents. A response rate of 68 percent of the superintendents showed that:

- 85.7 percent were male
- 84.2 percent were married
- 87.2 percent were between the ages of forty-six and sixty-five
- 50 percent were registered Democrats
- While 41 percent were in their first three years of service, 24 percent had served more than ten years
- 73 percent had an earned doctoral degree
- 74.3 percent were serving in school systems between 5,001 to 25,000 students
- 77.9 percent were serving in rural districts
- 56 percent had served in only one school district as superintendent
- 83.4 percent were serving in school districts where their board was between five and seven members in composition.

Wheeler wanted to know if the intersection of gender, age, and education was a significant factor in superintendent tenure. The results of his study are shown in table 5.1.

Table 5.1. The Statistically Significant Intersection of Gender, Age, and Education and Factors Associated with the Wheeler 2012 Study of Superintendent Turnover in North Carolina

Factor	Gender	Age	Education
Politics and/or bureaucracy	0	0	X
Receiving federal, state, or local mandates	0	0	0
Personnel matters	0	0	0
Leadership style	0	X	0
Superintendent experience	0	0	0
Fiscal restraints	0	0	X
Working with school board members	0	0	0
Dealing with legal action	0	0	0
Loss of personal time	0	0	0

Note: X = significant at .05 or better

Wheeler's respondents did not differ statistically by gender. But on matters of education and age there were statistically significant differences. This finding matches the notion of leadership as *accoutrements*. Age is connected with maturity and experience as well as leadership style, while education represents new knowledge to inform practice and by which to understand the collective challenges facing school systems, the most formidable of which pertained to educational finances and fiduciary constraints.

Table 5.2 is a more nuanced presentation of the factors which the sampled superintendents indicated led to job turnover. Wheeler (2012) only examined 61 percent of the total possible combinations and of these only seven (19 percent) were statistically significant. Board member pressure on superintendents within fiscal constraints mixed in with federal, state, or local mandates, and the politics dealing with the bureaucracy were potent factors in producing turnover.

Additional statistically significant factors were personnel issues and resolving differences with board members. The experience of the superintendent in dealing with these issues was also statistically significant.

The movement from management to leadership is what makes the concept of *accoutrement* a dynamic one. An accoutrement is never a permanent condition. Rather it is in the process of always becoming. In this sense, "great leadership" is never permanently "great." It is always rising successfully to meet the next challenge. And the reflection part of the *accoutrement* model is aptly summarized by George Orwell: "Every life viewed from the inside is a series of defeats" (*Wit and Wisdom*, 2012, p. 17).

We also see that leaders who today we call "great" had their moments of abject failure. Franklin Roosevelt took a beating by friend and foe alike over his efforts to pack the Supreme Court.

Winston Churchill resigned from his office as First Lord of the Admiralty and suffered for years over the failed attempt to open a second front in Turkey in World War I at Gallipoli. He was forced from office as the result of his misfortune and ate humble pie when he pleaded to be retained by saying, "I will accept any office—the lowest if you like—that you care to offer me" (Keegan, 2002, p. 87). Benjamin Franklin's "failures" in negotiating peace and keeping France on America's side in the conflict with England are also well documented in history (Morgan, 2002, p. 292).

Table 5.2. The Statistically Significant Interaction between Specific Factors and Challenges Confronting Superintendents Which Lead to Superintendent Turnover in the Wheeler 2012 Study

Factors	Dealing with Legal Action against Me	Dealing with Legal Action against the School District	Pressure from Board Members	Feeling a Great Deal Is Expected of Me	Resolving Differences with Board Members	Pressure from Board Members on Classroom Teachers
Politics and bureaucracy	0	0	X	X	N/A	N/A
Federal, state, local mandates	0	0	N/A	X	N/A	N/A
Personnel matters	0	0	N/A	N/A	X	N/A
Leadership style	0	0	N/A	N/A	N/A	N/A
Superintendent experience	0	0	N/A	N/A	N/A	X
Fiscal restraints	X	0	N/A	N/A	N/A	X
Working with school board members	0	0	N/A	N/A	N/A	N/A
Dealing with legal action	X	0	N/A	N/A	N/A	N/A
Loss of personal time	N/A	0	N/A	N/A	N/A	N/A

Note: X = statistically significant at .05 level or better

LEARNING HOW TO BECOME GREAT LEADERS

In a study conducted by Watkins (2012) of forty business executives in a variety of positions about what was different about "top leadership" or what was termed "enterprise leadership" from successful managerial implementation at lower levels in an organization, Watkins discovered what he labeled the "seven seismic shifts"(p. 66) when managers had to learn how to become leaders. We believe that Watkins's "seismic shifts" are simply examples of *accoutrements*. We show them here in a developmental sequence as applied to someone who has moved from a principalship to a superintendency in educational administration.

Of course, successful school unit leadership is also one of acquiring *accoutrements*, but as anyone who has actually done it successfully would say, it is a very different variety of *accoutrements* with a different mindset required. As a leader rises within an organization, the accompanying view and vision must change. This shift may or may not be seismic as Watkins terms it, but it may be radical for any one individual.

Success at one level in an organization does not guarantee success at another. Organizations contain within them a variety of climates and contexts. As experience, age/maturation, and education work together to sew a new garment, a revised *accoutrement* emerges. If it enables improved performance within a specific role, the result is enhanced and improved leadership. Table 5.3 provides an example.

Leithwood and Sun (2012) examined seventeen unpublished studies regarding transformational school leadership and which practices were common to all of those studies. The two most common elements were "setting directions—developing a widely shared vision/goals for the school/building consensus/inspirational motivation/charisma [and] developing people—providing individualized support and consideration" (p. 399). The first common element of setting directions is also reflected in the Watkins (2012) data, especially in moving from bricklayer to architect.

Great leadership is neither static nor solitary. It is a continuous act of reappraisal, reapproachment, revision, readjustment, reimagining, and revitalization, not to mention one of constant re-creation of self and identity over a career. John Gardner (1968) differentiates between "great leadership" and "excellent leadership," a useful distinction, we believe:

> Some people may have greatness thrust upon them. Very few have excellence thrust upon them. They achieve it. They do not achieve it unwit-

Table 5.3. The Movement from the Principalship to the Superintendency: An Example of Leadership Accoutrement

Accoutrement Dimension Derived from Watkins	Charting Movement in the Development of Leadership Accoutrements		
	Not Realized "Poor" Leadership	Partially Realized "Functional" Leadership	Fully Realized "Great" Leadership
Specialist to generalist	Cannot move from a view of subunit functions and applications to the total system.	Can adapt some school functions to larger district functions but not all.	Effective oversight of the full set of school district functions.
Analyst to integrator	Unable to rise above person-to-person supervision, namely, supervision of classroom teachers.	Can supervise some functions which are similar at the school, coordination of tests, and some others.	Is able to rise above individuals and focus on functions and the creation and integration of functional teams.
Tactician to strategist	Cannot rise above operational details on a day-to-day basis, tends to micromanagement.	Is able to discern some patterns and avoids getting bogged down in the day-to-day details.	Can identify critical patterns of operations and functions and not get bogged down in the operational details.
Bricklayer to architect	The mindset is that a system is essentially just a collection of subunits, i.e., a system of schools instead of a school system.	Understands that systems can be redesigned and begins to discern the principles and possible ways such a redesign could occur.	Develops a mindset which is that of system architect in which strategies, structures, and processes are integrated and applied to schools.
Problem solver to agenda setter	Used to try to resolve problems and fix things one by one on a case-by-case basis; some problems never get solved, and some of these are critical.	Begins to sort problems in various ways and to relate how they may be resolved using common tactics.	Understands that the top role is not to solve problems but to determine which problems are to be solved.
Warrior to diplomat	Approaches day-to-day work as putting together pep talks to get staff members to go into organizational combat.	Uses some different approaches in forming and maintaining effective relationships and teams.	Uses a variety of interpersonal tools such as persuasion, conflict management and resolution, building coalitions.
Supporting cast member to lead role	Difficult to think about performing the role without being a member of a group of principals.	Is able to rise above former subunit role and grow into a larger, broader level of responsibilities.	Works through channels, understands the importance of vision and role modeling.

tingly, by "doing what comes naturally"; and they don't stumble into it in the course of amusing themselves. All excellence involves discipline and tenacity of purpose. (p. 66)

We think *great leaders* show a lifetime propensity of hard work, discipline, and tenacity of purpose. Greatness is defined by achievement, largely in difficult circumstances.

However, the key behind the interaction of the *accoutering* process is doubt. Doubt is one of the most powerful forces for change. The process of change begins first in the mind and then moves into action later. Change begins with the idea that the status quo is not acceptable for whatever reason. Hecht (2003) put it succinctly:

The history of doubt looks different than other histories, because it highlights what goes on between periods of certainty; it's like seeing a map upside down—it takes time for the new contours to take shape. The history of being awake to certain contradictions of our condition is the negative image of the history of certainty. (pp. 1–2)

Great educational leaders have come to doubt contemporary thinking and practice. Their doubt fuels their efforts to change and confront the certainty of the moment. All change, then, begins with the inner questioning of the leader. Such questioning always takes courage. The words of Albert Schweitzer (1965) present a trenchant summary:

Those who vow to do good should not expect people to clear the stones from their path on this account. They must expect the contrary: that others will roll great boulders down upon them. Such obstacles can be overcome only by the kind of strength gained in the very struggle. Those who merely resent obstacles will waste whatever force they have. (p. 44)

CHAPTER LEARNING EXTENSIONS

Testing Your Understanding of This Chapter about Identity

Look over the matrix in table 5.4 and compare your understanding to those of the authors. Remember that your response should be two edged; that is, how it looks gazing through the lens of the chapter and then a second skeptical examination of the lens itself. Remember that your values, knowledge, and skills create your identity.

Table 5.4. What Do You Believe about Identity?

Statement	What do you think? True/false? Yes/no?	Where you are in your understanding
5.1. Leaders stand apart from followers.		
5.2. Leadership that is logical and rational avoids excessive emotional appeal.		
5.3. Once constructed in childhood, human identity remains constant throughout life.		
5.4. Leadership is best studied within a social science perspective.		
5.5. Great leaders handle defeats differently than others.		

6

THE CONTINUING QUEST TO DISCERN LEADERSHIP CONTOURS

Somewhere, something incredible is waiting to be known.

—Carl Sagan (1934–1996)

Over the years, the search for best practices in schools and for best practices for leaders to exhibit has been fraught with difficulties (Papa, 2011, August). The effective schools movement of over forty years ago brought the inevitable question of the definition of effective. Is it test scores? Which ones? Is it the national Common Core Standards, state standards, textbook specific standards, and so on? That issue has not been universally solved.

Concomitant issues were those politically based "best" (e.g., immersion versus bilingual language programs, etc.), "statistically significant" practices where large sample sizes made the smallest of gains or program differences "significantly" better and put best practices in context (for whom, poor children, gifted children, etc.).

The line of inquiry for this book essentially began in 1999 with a two-year study of high achieving, high minority population schools in California. The results of that study formed the basis of the book *Leadership on Purpose: Promising Practices for African American and Hispanic Students* (Papa [Papalewis] & Fortune, 2002).

From the original study, ongoing research focused on fifteen best practices in middle/junior and senior high school and ten best practices in elementary schools. Those best practices were a combination of values, knowledge, and skill/site practices utilized by leaders in the California schools studied.

Beginning in 2009 these best practices were incorporated into a questionnaire that was given to superintendents at their annual fall conferences, respectively 2010 and 2011, and during site focus groups, including the four identified high achieving schools in Arizona (see appendix B), and at several principal-in-training graduate courses. Superintendents responded to both the elementary and junior/middle/high school practices, as did principals and principals-in-training to their respective site level. A brief summary of each of the studies and their respective results appears below.

CHRONOLOGY OF THE LINE OF INQUIRY

Exemplary urban schools that defied the downward achievement trends at the turn of the twenty-first century were the focus of the original study. A two-year research study was done to understand what made the difference in thirteen identified high-performing African American and Hispanic majority schools. After extensive interviews and observations, the study found these school principals and teachers believed and expected that all students were capable of learning and went about creating high-achievement learning environments. A full description of the study can be found in the Papa [Papalewis] and Fortune (2002) book.

California had recently initiated a comprehensive accountability system for its public schools. The accountability system led to a school-by-school score to a ranking system called the Academic Performance Index (API). The API was the cornerstone of the Public Schools Accountability Act (California Senate Bill 1X) signed into law April 1999 (California Department of Education, 2001).

The statewide rank was used that compared an individual school's API to all of the schools in its grade-level category statewide. With respect to all elementary, middle, or high schools, the rank is interpreted as a range: 9 or 10 ranked well above average; 7 or 8 above average; 5 or 6 about average; 3 or 4 below average; and 1 or 2 well below average.

Overall, for schools with 50+ percent African American students, only 16 of 125 had API scores greater than 7. For schools with 50+ percent Hispanic students, only 157 of 2,209 had API scores greater than 7.

The thirteen schools visited had the following baseline API score rankings: API 10—one Hispanic elementary; API 9—one African American elementary school; API 8—one Hispanic elementary, two African American elementary; API 7—two Hispanic elementary, one African American elementary, one African American K–8; API 6—three African American (elementary, middle school, and high school).

A total of nine team members were trained with respect to qualitative participatory research methods. A team of five researchers went to each school site. Of the team members, four visited all the schools. Besides the two authors, Papa and Fortune (superintendent from a suburban school district and university professor), three of the researchers were current district office directors or recent past principals. Most had worked in both urban and suburban schools with thirty-plus years of experience in teaching and/or administration.

The ten elementary practices and the fifteen postelementary (middle/high school) practices formed the basis for the continued line of inquiry. These appear below. The overall results were summarized in the aforementioned book.

Best Practices in High-Performing Elementary Schools

1. Structured high expectations
2. Manipulate the length of day and school year to get more time for students who need it
3. Direct instruction methods utilized
4. Use of reading coaches
5. Frequent and multiple levels of assessment practices
6. Teach and practice throughout year test-taking strategies
7. Solid teacher communication across grade levels
8. Teachers know the standards and tie them to lesson plans
9. Solid English language development programs
10. Students are expected to respect teachers

Best Practices in High-Performing Middle/Junior and High Schools

1. Strong uniform dress code required
2. Principal is highly visible

3. Structured high expectations
4. Manipulate the length of day and school year for students
5. Parents involved in SAT preparation
6. Teachers/principal/parents trained with students for SAT prep
7. Daily uninterrupted sustained reading for fifteen minutes
8. Content Standards posted in each classroom
9. Portfolios are kept for all students
10. Counselor on site, and ties to community services
11. Suggestion box for students that principal responds to each suggestion
12. Scheduling fits needs of courses, students, and teachers for maximum flexibility
13. No early release for juniors and seniors
14. Full-time technologist to service computers
15. Classrooms show evidence of celebrating diversity

These identified promising or best practices listed above were further developed through chronological, peer-reviewed research in the development of the concept of *accoutrements*. As noted in the citations listed in appendix C, the line of inquiry continued through other writings.

THE FUTURE DEMOGRAPHICS OF AMERICA: MICROCOSM ARIZONA

In 2009, planning began for a field-based study of Arizona schools utilizing the data from the California study and current literature in the field. Arizona was chosen for a variety of reasons. One prominent reason was the sense that Arizona is a snapshot of what the future holds for many states.

- Arizona's children are less like adults here in race and ethnicity than in any state in the nation, citing an analysis of the 2010 census (Hansen, 2011, p. B6):
  - 63 percent of adults with just 42 percent who are seventeen years or younger are non-Hispanic White;
  - Following behind Arizona are Nevada and New Mexico;
  - Tucson leads the nation with a 25 percent difference between percentages of adults and children who are non-Hispanic White. Phoenix ranks fourth in the country;

- As of 2010, California, Hawaii, New Mexico, and Texas were majority minority, meaning that less than half the population were non-Hispanic Whites; and
- The nation will become majority-minority by 2042 and children by 2023. (Hansen, 2011, p. B6)
- Statewide 57 percent of students are eligible for free and reduced-price lunches (Faller, 2012):
  - A child qualifies if a family of four earns $29,055 or less for a free meal;
  - A child from a family of four that makes less than $41,438 a year qualifies for a reduced-price lunch; and
  - The federal government pays districts for students' free lunches and covers the difference for those who are charged a reduced price. (Faller, 2012, p. B2)
- One of five Arizona children is being raised in a home where the head of household is not a high school graduate, a living situation that could have dire implications for the state because research shows that parental education, occupation, and income all impact children's school readiness and academic performance. (Aztalk, 2011, B11)
- According to a recent Kids Count report, Arizona ranks fifth worst among states on this measure. (Britz, 2011, p. B4)
- According to 2010 figures by the Arizona Charter Schools Association, Chandler city has 25 percent of its students in charters. (Britz, 2011, p. B4)
- Arizona 2020 ABOR report 2008 has a 56 percent graduation rate. (Koebler, 2011)

High achieving Arizona public schools face the reality of the above demographics while existing within a ground zero of what some have been termed extreme politics.

Arizona Superintendents

At two statewide superintendent conferences (2010 and 2011), data relating to the best practices noted earlier in this chapter was gathered (n = 51) of primarily superintendents and a few assistant superintendents. These fifty-one district leaders were asked to rank the ten elementary practices and the fifteen middle/high school practices that had been identified in the original study in California in terms of the effect on supporting high achievement.

For elementary school achievement, four top practices emerged from the rankings. They included structured high expectations; teachers know the standards and tie them to learning plans; frequent and multiple levels of assessment practices; and solid teacher communication across grade levels. For the middle/high school ratings, three items emerged as highest ranked. They were structured high expectations; principal is highly visible; and scheduling fits the needs of courses, students, and teachers for maximum flexibility.

Principals-in-Training

In fall 2010 and spring 2011, students preparing to be elementary school principals responded to the elementary best practices, while those preparing for postelementary principals completed the middle/junior/high school version.

For those pursuing the elementary principalship (n = 89), the top four best practices were structured high expectations; teachers know the standards and tie them to lesson plans; high engagement of students (added); and teachers' use of research-based teaching practices (added). For those pursuing postelementary assignments (n = 76), the top best practices were structured high expectations; principal is highly visible; high student engagement (added); and scheduling to fit the needs of students (for remediation or enrichment).

Arizona High Achieving Schools Administrator Focus Groups

During 2011, four high achieving school districts in Arizona were identified using the state education database, which ranks districts based upon their performance using state-defined measures of success that follow NCLB. A brief description of these districts can be found in appendix B. The total number of participants in the focus groups were fifty-six (n = 56) and included superintendents and their administrative teams (principals and district-level leaders). The team of researchers consisted of the four Arizona coauthors.

The prompts used with the focus groups were (1) What would you say are the key components of your district's academic success? (2) Describe your personal leadership characteristics. (3) Describe leadership style as it relates to student individual differences. (4) Can you point to specific leadership practices that have contributed to students' academic success? Additionally, these focus groups took the same survey noted above given at the superintendent conferences. The prompt follow-up from the survey was (1) What practice was most important to you? And, what practice was the least important to you?

The four top practices ranked by these district-level elementary administrators were structured high expectations; frequent and multiple levels of assessment; teachers know the standards and tie them to lesson plans; and direct instructional practices utilized. For the middle/high school district-level administrators, the top four practices ranked were principal is highly visible; structured high expectations; scheduling fits the needs of students, courses, and teachers for maximum flexibility; and content standards were posted in each classroom.

As noted previously, the line of inquiry which lead to the identification of leadership, the *accoutrements* (see appendix C), began with the 1999–2001 research study in California schools. As was seen with the more recent Arizona studies, top-ranked practices were the broader values, knowledges, and skills practiced rather than specific site programs mentioned. This line of inquiry led to the identification of leadership as *accoutrements*.

THE QUEST OF IDENTITY THROUGH THE CONTOURS OF LEADERSHIP

Distinguishing "poor" to "functional" to "great" leadership is the focus of this book. The empirical research over a fourteen-year period led to identifying effective leadership characteristics called *accoutrements*. As noted in previous chapters, these are those *special characteristics and skills* that the leaders of high achieving schools possess and actively display, which lead to high achieving students and effective, replicative programs.

Embedded in the *accoutrements* are the values, knowledge, and skills the "great" leader reflects on and is reflexive in a continuing quest to understand his/her identity within the contour of district or school site setting. The use of the term *accoutrements* is purposeful, as it gives emphasis to the ever changing of the "clothes" we wear as teachers, assistant principals, principals, and superintendents. The addition of a new part of our identity bears both reflection and reflexion.

1. Leading Adult Learners

Leaders should know adult learners learn on a need-to-know basis (Papa & Papa, 2011). Adults learn differently and want what they want when they want it. Fairness for the adult learner takes the learner at his/her particular learning point. Thus, the superintendent must know how to work with the principals for program implementation, and the principals must know the program and know how to work with teachers to achieve the program goals. Both the superintendent and principals must be going in the same direction and know the teachers and students to be able to move forward.

2. Developing Compassion as Human Agency

Leaders know one-size-fits-all does not work. The totality of our boards', teachers', and students' mental, physical, and spiritual aspects is the package that must be taken into perspective. How better to understand human agency? We must ensure the future school leader has a varied repertoire of fair and just behaviors. The "great" leader knows how to approach individuals and knows what they need to excel.

3. Acknowledging Ignored but Intended Skills

Leaders know how to listen. We know it is vital for the socially just *activist* leader to be caring and compassionate. Vision building requires it. Strong personnel relations demand it and have the understanding that it is okay and normal to wrestle with complex issues. Honesty is key, as is a good sense of humor.

4. Encouraging Intellectual Curiosity

Leaders are curious. We can prepare school leaders to be curious of their school setting. Curiosity in learning and how it is fostered in the school environment is critical for school staff to develop, understand, and apply. Curiosity is fairness in action, as it asks "why" with no assigning of blame.

Is the leader willing to suspend his or her own perceptions/biases to examine new ideas? Is the leader willing to let others take a leadership role? Is the leader willing to give credit to others to stimulate collaboration? Is ongoing knowledge acquisition encouraged through the study of research?

5. Understanding Futurity

Leaders know technology can give us a false sense that it should be easier to solve the problems we face within our schools than it really is while providing supposed efficiencies. Leaders must be exposed to learning frames that go against the grain of current wisdom.

Going against the grain may just be the best leader trait we can encourage. More importantly, where are we going? What might the future landscape look like? For example, before selecting computer hardware and software, much thought should be given to sustainability and budget refreshment.

6. Exploring Imaginativeness

Leaders are creative, inspiring, original, resourceful, visionary, artistic, inventive, and ingenious. These are the synonyms of imaginative leadership. One's values, knowledge, and skills shape our experiences. Exploration with a good heart, an almost spiritual need to be of service to others, to be the hope for others, to help others be all they can be, and to see the good in others is limited only by one's lack of imagination. [A more full description of these six *accoutrements* can be found in the Rowman & Littlefield 2012 book *Educational Leadership at 2050*, pp. 72–78.]

Elliot Eisner (2005) describes the imaginative life as

> one built out of experience. One would think, given the importance of imagination, that it would be regarded as one of the basics of education. It is not on anyone's list of basics, at least not in any national report on the state of our schools. (p. 108)

He continues that "we are far more concerned with the correct replication of what already exists than with cultivating the posers of innovation or the celebration of thinking" (p. 108).

These *accoutrements* reflect values and the knowledge base of effective administrators that are then manifested in skills and site practices. From a leadership perspective, it is important to note that one's values and knowl-edge drive the skills/practices; that is, skills/practices are site specific.

An example is proffered utilizing *accoutrement* one, *understanding the adult learner* (Papa & Papa, 2011). If a leader values individual differences and understands that adult learners vary in their learning styles, a team approach (several differing styles) to professional development might be a practice utilized. However, if only the team approach is presented as ef-fective, a leader may miss the point of representing varying learner styles and do a one-style-fits-all.

These *accoutrements* go beyond the basic requirements of a leader's position. These are those *special characteristics and skills* that through application and practice are sewn into one's persona. These are the ac-cessories that separate the great leaders from the rest (Papa, 2011; Papa, 2012; Papa & English, 2011).

Another example comes from the focus groups of the *accoutrements* in practice—specific skills that could be learned and transferred across per-sonnel and districts. The session started with a straightforward prompt that asked what makes this school exemplary as noted by the State of Arizona. The initial response from a principal, seconded by all, was the established culture focused on student learning and collegial support.

When asked for specificity, what emerged were specific practices that promoted that culture. For example, at district meetings communication is emphasized with each administrative team member sharing assessments of his/her school, using data to talk about achievement, student issues, parent issues, and so on (*Human agency and ignored intended skills*). Their focus is on where they are now and where they want to go (*Futurity*).

In addition, these principals were encouraged by their superintendent to seek literature on relevant topics and provided a budget to explore alter-native solutions to student learning outcomes (*Intellectual curiosity*). They undergo the same professional development as the teachers with respect to instructional tools (*Adult learners*) and are encouraged and supported to build personal relationships with their students, staffs, and parents to make it easier and more productive in the work environment (*Human agency*).

As well, they spend two days a week as instructional leader. Their vis-ibility in classrooms is deemed essential, as is their activity in instruction (*Imaginativeness*).

During those two days of each week, the superintendent doesn't involve them in administration, except in emergencies (*Adult learners*). In sum, these public school leaders feel professional and responsible. It is clear that the basics of management (budgets, discipline, personnel, etc.) are "givens" rather than purely administrative priorities that are their only tasks.

As noted previously, this is where the *accoutrements* (Papa, 2011; Papa, 2011, May) take a first step in that direction. The assumption is that anyone going for the superintendency has mastered the basics through training and/or experience at the principalship level. Then the specifics of *accoutrements* kick in: understanding the adult learner; sense of human agency (fair and just behaviors toward all); ignored intended skills (listening, mentoring, reflecting); intellectual curiosity; futurity; and imaginativeness.

The work continues to more specifically define these skills and their ability to be amplified and transferred through application and practice. Based on fourteen years of research, the characteristics and skills of the *accoutrements* are related to actual examples covering curriculum, pedagogically focused teacher professional development, parent and community relations, and especially, all aspects of student achievement (English, Papa, Mullen, & Creighton, 2012). A scale is under construction and being field tested (for more information contact Dr. Papa at Rosemary.Papa@nau.edu).

How we lead our schools is the performance of our skills. Why we lead our schools is linked to our identity and values. When we study and do research, we build our knowledge base. All of these shape our identity continuum. Eisner (2005) asks, "Can our education system flourish without losers? Is it possible for us to frame conceptions of education and society that rest on more generous assumptions?" (p. 171).

These are the questions "great" leaders grapple with daily.

CHAPTER LEARNING EXTENSIONS

Testing Your Understanding of This Chapter about Contours

We know that by now you know the drill. Look over the matrix in table 6.1. Remember that your response should be two edged; that is, how it looks gazing through the lens of the chapter and then a second skeptical examination of the lens itself. Research is essential to be both reflective and reflexive. Your identity is composed of the *accoutrements* and more—the more is what you must discern.

Table 6.1.   What Do You Believe about Contours?

Great Leader Statements	What do you think? True/false? Yes/no?	Where you are in your understanding
6.1. Leaders understand and practice adult learning skills.		
6.2. Leadership is honest.		
6.3. Leaders should follow current wisdom.		
6.4. Leadership is social justice in action.		
6.5. Research is necessary for identity and leadership.		

Appendix A

LEARNING EXTENSIONS
AUTHORS' COMMENTARY

These are the responses of the authors to the statements at the end of each of the chapters. They can be compared to the reader's judgment and test of his/her own understanding. The authors encourage additional reading and thought about them.

CHAPTER I

1.1   Leadership is interactional in a social construction between followers and leaders and exists within a culture, context, and linguistic conventions which are arbitrary but common to both parties.

1.2   Identity is constructed by interacting with others, from family and extended family first, and then through peers, even by those hostile to us in rival families, clans, or groups. An individual also has multiple identities. A woman may be a wife within a family and a mother, but in the work world a boss, both with a different identity. The notion of "nested identities" is a way to think about identity.

1.3   Leadership does involve reflective thinking, but that is not enough. Reflective thinking too often does not examine what it is that is being "reflected upon," only if certain targets were reached and what obstacles were in the way and how to overcome them if encountered again.

1.4   The nature of reflexive thinking is to think about how one is thinking. It is raising the issue of how the leader is thinking about something, as this defines the problem and determines what appropriate solutions are. To use a somewhat well-worn phrase, it is "stepping out of the box" and looking at how one was considering a problem in the box.

1.5   Heroic leadership still has adherents, but it has given way to "heroic actions," which means having the courage to move against complicated and entrenched issues. Distributed leadership means taking certain duties and breaking them up and assigning them to different individuals. The use of distributed leadership may not change a hierarchy of command or anyone's actual role, though it may alter individual job descriptions. If one is after more democratic and/or collaborative schools or school systems, distributed leadership is no guarantee that greater democracy or collaboration may be the result.

CHAPTER 2

2.1   Leadership as an *accoutrement* is continuously developed. It is interactive and complex. Habits of reflexivity, reflection, and honest self-assessment model the core values that lead to leader success.

2.2   Successful school system officials believe that investment in people is what education is about. They believe schools exist to serve the community. Leaders build a shared focus on doing what's best for students, and that drives decisions of all sides. They espouse the notion that *we are all in this together to achieve our goals.*

2.3   There is no one "correct" way to run a school or a school system. So much is centered in context and culture. The key to addressing the challenges to student success in each school community lies within the creativity of that school community. In building high expectations, decisions must be made that support instruction and a commitment to all students' success. This is not a process for wimps. It takes hard work, long hours, and cooperation of all community members.

2.4   A common language to describe a school's vision and mission keeps the team on the same page. Jargon and slogans take on special meaning to all members of the community, often providing a shortcut to clear understanding. Dialogue among members grows deeper, more meaningful, and protects decisions from misinterpretations.

2.5   The primary purpose of schools is to educate students, which is done through effective curriculum and instruction. Effective faculty development is based on the importance of continually improving instruction. Building high expectations for instruction creates a "culture of instruction" through peer pressure to excel. Creating multiple levels of leadership to that end stimulates teachers professionally.

CHAPTER 3

3.1   It is a truism that leaders have to be born, and so the statement has to be true by definition. However, leadership is a co-construction between leaders and followers involving common aspirations of causes impacting both.

3.2   True self-knowledge is extremely difficult to accomplish because it has to confront essential truisms that a person has come to accept in the past. These have to be reconsidered, because one becomes skeptical of every past belief and assumption. Some of these have been set in childhood and have come to be the core of a person.

3.3   Knowledge turns to dogma when it cannot be questioned and is not recognized as a construct built on assumptions which may be false.

3.4   "Research based" covers a lot of ground and can hide a whole lot of problems and false conclusions. Very little research is conclusive as a single-shot study. One must know something about the quality of the researchers, the methods employed, the conditions of the study, the context of the study, and importantly what was *not* studied.

3.5   It is not about ignorance versus knowledge. Rather it is about how knowledge exists within hierarchies of power, and therefore it benefits some more than others. Knowledge is therefore only power to those who use it as an extension of their influence with extant social hierarchies.

CHAPTER 4

4.1   The "managerial trap" awaits every unsuspecting leader. It is all too easy to get caught up in the notion that the leader's job is to leave at the end of the day with an empty in-basket. However, the work of schools centers on learning, and school leaders must develop craft knowledge in how learning occurs. Principals and others must see themselves as "lead learners."

4.2　Creating effective, high achieving schools or school districts is contingent on creating a mission that is easily understood and can be translated into contingent and connected actions at each level in the organization. To effectively build such connections requires leaders with both personal integrity and the skills needed to inspire others.

4.3　School leaders are bombarded with questions, information, and acting on unmet needs. Effective leaders are self-disciplined and selective. The habit of self-reflection can be very useful in refining one's ability to maintain a disciplined focus. Honestly answering the question, *How does what I am doing right now contribute to our goals?* is a good first step.

4.4　Effective leaders do not simply stop being "managers." Instead they develop efficiencies, by recognizing that time needs to be set aside for both (a) making the trains run on time and (b) making sure they are going in the right direction; by creating specific processes for routine tasks; and by using technology to expand communication and influence.

4.5　Personal and organizational efficacy grows from a belief that one's actions can produce results. Optimism is about embracing both failure and progress, and recognizing that the latter cannot happen without the former.

CHAPTER 5

5.1　Leaders stand with followers, not apart from them. No followers, no leaders. Leadership is relational between followers and leaders.

5.2　Effective leadership always involves the full range of human emotion. Some discourses are less emotional than others. Scientific discourse relies heavily on logic and reason rather than political rhetoric.

5.3　Some aspects of identity appear to be more stable than others. Since identity is socially and culturally constructed, much of it remains unconscious to an individual.

5.4　Social science models are limited in what they can tell us about leadership. Such models leave much of what constitutes leadership such as questions of morality and goodness out of their lens. To fully understand leadership requires the presence of the arts as well as science.

5.5　Great leaders are more resilient than more ordinary ones. Their resiliency can be attributed to a variety of factors including absolute faith in their cause.

CHAPTER 6

6.1   It's important that leaders work with adults as adults and don't view them as simply grown-up children. Since schools work with children and young adults, it is too easy to adopt a "parent-child" relationship with adults in the school. An "adult to adult" relationship means one of mutual respect and collaborative, collegial interaction. It is too easy to fall into a hierarchical trap in schools and school systems. Working with people as people and not a commanding, bureaucratic structure is essential to creating an intellectually stimulating and open climate workplace.

6.2   Well, this sounds like a platitude, and who could disagree with this statement? Honesty has many dimensions, however. Perhaps the most honest thing leaders can do is to be positive within the constraints in which they work while still remaining skeptical about "instant cures" or the latest "fad" being adopted. Honesty also requires one to be reflexive about how one has chosen to work toward problem solutions by defining a problem one way and not another. It also means one has to be constantly alert to seeing data and results in different ways.

Thus, honesty means a perpetual vigilance about anything that is taken for granted or assumed to be so. At times this posture can be unsettling, and the tension it creates within a leader has to be managed. There has to be strong internal discipline to live on the edge of certainty and doubt.

6.3   The current wisdom is merely the latest "whiz bang" or "cure" being discussed. In some ways it's much like reading about a new diet that works for some movie star flashed in the supermarket tabloids. Leaders have to remain grounded and look for data from methods and means that have been subjected to longitudinal analyses in solid research reports. However, even research itself often suffers from acute myopia, and it too has to be examined very carefully.

6.4   Social justice is based on the recognition that neither schools nor society spread their advantages equally among all classes of people. The linkage between those who are not doing well in schools also representing those who generally are not doing well in the larger society is well known. Great leaders fully understand the challenges in creating level playing fields for all children not only within their schools but in the larger society. This recognition propels great leaders to also be political activists in arenas beyond their schools.

6.5   While research is welcomed on new notions of identity, identity itself has to be subjected to a fresh look. Great leaders have many faces. Context determines which face is best suited to specific circumstances. The idea of "nested identities" fits the requirements of having to work effectively within many contexts.

Appendix B

A BRIEF DESCRIPTION OF THE CONTEXTS OF GREAT LEADERSHIP

CASA GRANDE ELEMENTARY SCHOOL DISTRICT
www.cgelem.k12.az.us

The Casa Grande Elementary School District encompasses an area of 400 square miles, including the city of Casa Grande and surrounding agricultural and tribal lands in western Pinal County, Arizona. It is located midway between Phoenix and Tucson, at the junction of Interstates 8 and 10. During the 2011–2012 school year, the district served approximately 7,300 students in nine elementary schools and three middle schools.

For the last half of the twentieth century, the district grew slowly but steadily. Then, during the residential housing boom of the last decade, growth accelerated rapidly, resulting in the construction of four new schools between 2001 and 2007. During the economic downturn from 2008 to 2012, enrollment declined by approximately 8 percent as regional unemployment rates climbed. Enrollment growth is expected to return as the state and national economies recover.

The district was selected for this study due to improvements in student achievement over time. For example, in 2000, 33 percent of students performed at grade level on state reading assessments; by 2011, this percentage had climbed to 75 percent. According to a 2011 performance audit by the Arizona auditor general, the district outperformed demographically similar peer districts. In the state's 2011 accountability system, the district received a "B" rating and was ranked in the top quartile of all school districts in the state.

In 2011–2012, the student population was 60 percent Latino, 24 percent White, 6 percent Native American, 4 percent African American, and 1 percent Asian. In October 2011, the state reported that 74 percent of the district's students were socioeconomically disadvantaged.

CRANE ELEMENTARY SCHOOL DISTRICT
www.craneschools.org

The Crane Elementary School District is located near the southwest corner of the state, which shares borders with California and Mexico. The district, established in 1899, covers forty-four square miles of southwest Yuma County and includes a total population of approximately 45,000. It serves the western part of the city of Yuma and the bordering regions, which are primarily agricultural.

The district has eight elementary schools, serving grades kindergarten through six, and two middle schools, serving grades seven and eight. In 2011–2012, the district's enrollment was approximately 6,200. After years of steady enrollment growth, enrollment began a slight period of decline in recent years. Enrollment is expected to stabilize in the coming years (Arizona School Facilities Board, 2011).

The district was selected for this study because of its tradition of outperforming peer districts with similar demographics. The district performs at or near state averages in reading and mathematics on state assessments, and well above the performance of districts similar in size and population. In 2011, the district received a "B" rating and was ranked in the top quartile of all school districts in the state in the state's accountability system (Arizona Department of Education, 2011).

The student population in the district is diverse. Seventy-four percent of students are identified as socioeconomically disadvantaged. In 2011–2012, the student population was 80 percent Latino, 16 percent White, 2 percent African American, 1 percent Native American, and 1 percent Asian (Crane Schools, 2011).

GLENDALE UNION HIGH SCHOOL DISTRICT
www.guhsdaz.org

The Glendale Union High School District serves students in grades 9 through 12 in Glendale and north Phoenix, and has done so for over 100 years. In the 2011–2012 school year, the district had an enrollment of approximately 15,000 students. As the Phoenix metropolitan area grew rapidly during the three decades following World War II, this growth had a substantial impact on the district. In recent years, student enrollment has begun to decline, and a gradual decline is projected to continue in the coming years as residential neighborhoods age (Arizona School Facilities Board, 2011).

Like the other districts selected for this study, the district has a history of high student achievement in comparison to peer districts serving comparable populations. The district received an "A" rating from the Arizona Department of Education in the 2010–2011 school year. Four individual schools also received an "A" rating. These ratings are primarily based on overall achievement and growth in student achievement. Also included in this determination are other factors including the dropout rate, the graduation rate, and the rate by which English language learners become proficient in English (Arizona Department of Education, 2011).

The district has nine comprehensive high schools and two alternative campuses. As of October 2011, 59 percent of the students in the district were identified as socioeconomically disadvantaged. Fifty percent of the students in the district were identified as White, 36 percent were identified as Latino, 8 percent were identified as African American, 4 percent were identified as Asian, and 2 percent were identified as American Indian (Johnson, 2012).

VAIL UNIFIED SCHOOL DISTRICT
www.vail.k12.az.us

Located southeast of Tucson, the Vail district grew dramatically in recent decades, with enrollment booming from approximately 1,000 students in 1990 to a current enrollment of well over 10,000 students. Given its location and proximity to a major employment corridor, the district is expected to continue growing in the coming years. Vail has seven elementary schools, four middle schools, two comprehensive high schools, an alternative high school, and two charter schools (Arizona School Facilities Board, 2011).

All four of the study districts have a history of stability in district leadership. However, the Vail schools have enjoyed the greatest stability in the superintendent's office, with the current individual completing his twenty-sixth year in this position in the 2011–2012 school year.

Vail was selected for this study due to its exceptional achievement and its record of creativity and innovation. In the 2011 state accountability rankings, Vail enjoyed the distinction of being ranked as Arizona's top school district. The district received an "A" rating from the Arizona Department of Education in the 2010–2011 school year. All but two of the district's individual schools also received an "A" rating (Arizona Department of Education, 2011).

As of October 2011, 23 percent of the students in the district were identified as socioeconomically disadvantaged. Fifty-five percent of the students in the district were identified as White, 26 percent were identified as Latino, 4 percent were identified as African American, 2 percent were identified as Asian, and 1 percent were identified as American Indian (Baker, 2012).

Appendix C

A CHRONOLOGY OF PEER-REVIEWED RESEARCH ON THE *ACCOUTREMENTS*

Dr. Papa's line of inquiry which has led to the identification of leadership as *accoutrements* began with her university tenure (1986). Since 1986, following this line of inquiry as an organizational theorist—one's research that focuses on the individual within the organization and their relationships— she has presented/vetted in the following professional *blind peer-review* venues: International (n = 3); AERA (n = 8); NCPEA (n = 9); UCEA (n = 2); AASCU (n = 1); other state or regional (n = 2). Prior to 1986, craft knowledge experiences include teaching at the elementary and middle/high school levels, principalships, and chief school administrator positions.

REFERENCES

Papa, R., & Brown, R. (2011, November). *English language policy in Arizona schools: Blind to its own blindness.* Poster presentation at the Language, Education and Diversity Conference, University of Auckland, New Zealand.

English, F., Papa, R., Mullen, C., Creighton, T., & Berry, J. (2011, November). *Reverse casting educational leadership at the mid-century: Evocations of time travel.* A presentation—fireside chats at the annual conference of the University Council of Educational Administration, Pittsburgh, PA.

Papa, R., Culver, M., & Schwanenberger, M. (2011, August). *12 year empirical study on school leader best practices.* National Council of Professors of Educational Administration Annual Conference, Portland, OR.

English, F., Papa, R., & Mullen, C. (2011, August). *Blazing new trails: Preparing leaders for improving access and equity in tomorrow's schools.* National Council of Professors of Educational Administration Annual Conference, Portland, OR.

Papa, R., Culver, M., & Schwanenberger, M. (2011, April). *Leadership characteristics to turn around underperforming schools: Empirical research update.* Arizona Professors of Educational Administration, Annual Conference, Phoenix, AZ.

Papa, R., & Brown, R. (2011, January). *Leadership characteristics to turn around underperforming schools.* International Conference on Education, Honolulu, HI.

Brown, R., & Papa, R. (2008, February). *What they don't teach you at the summer leadership institutes.* Presentation at the American Association of State Colleges and Universities winter meeting, Tempe, AZ.

Papa, R. (Panel organizer). (2007, November). *Updating the national standards for school leaders.* University Council of Educational Administration, Annual conference, Washington, DC.

Papa, R., Loeffler, C., & Creighton, T. (2006). The relationship of adult learning styles and success in online graduate education. Presentation at the annual conference of the American Educational Research Association, San Francisco.

Loeffler, C., Creighton, T., & Papa, R. (2005). *Virtual success: The relationship of adult learning styles and success in online graduate education leadership programs.* Presentation at the annual conference of the National Council of Professors of Educational Administration Summit on the Preparation of School Leaders, Washington, DC.

Papa [Papalewis], R., & Fortune, R. (2003). *Promising site leadership practices for schools with African-American and Latino Students.* At the annual conference of the National School Boards Association, San Francisco.

Papa [Papalewis], R. (2002). *Promising leadership practices for principals.* Paper presented at the annual conference of the National Council of Professors of Educational Administration, Burlington, VT.

Papa [Papalewis], R., & Lee, E. *Promising site leadership practices for African-American and Latino Students.* (2002). At the annual conference of American Educational Research Association, New Orleans, LA.

Papa [Papalewis], R., & Kramer, G. L. (2002). *Mentoring, advising, and supporting students.* National Conference on Higher Education Communities of Practice, American Educational Research Association, Chicago, IL.

Papa [Papalewis], R., & Brown, R. (1998). *Leadership required for the new millennium.* Paper presented at the annual conference of the National Council of Professors of Educational Administration, Juneau, AK.

Papa [Papalewis], R. (1998). *Promising practices in educational administration programs.* Discussant for SIG/Teaching in Educational Administration at the annual conference of the American Educational Research Association Conference, San Diego, CA.

Papa [Papalewis], R. (1991). *Preparing school administrators for the culturally and linguistically diverse: A formal mentor training program in progress.* Paper presented at the annual conference of the American Educators Research Association, Chicago, IL. *(Resources in Education ED 333 094).*

Papa [Papalewis], R. (1990). *What we are becoming we are: Educational administration for the 21st Century.* Paper presented at the annual conference of the National Council of Professors of Educational Administration, Los Angeles, CA. (*Resources in Education ED 328 166*).

Papa [Papalewis], R. (1989). *A national challenge: The underrepresented in education.* Paper presented at the annual conference of the National Council of Professors of Educational Administration, Birmingham, AL.

Papa [Papalewis], R., & Brown, R. (1989). *Gender communication style and student evaluation of instruction.* Colloquium, University of Sydney, Australia.

Papa [Papalewis], R. (1989). *Gender characteristics of teaching and evaluation measures of instruction.* Presentation at the annual conference of the American Educational Research Association, San Francisco, CA.

Papa [Papalewis], R. (1988). *Artistry through symbolic language.* Paper presented at the annual conference of the National Council of Professors of Educational Administration, Kalamazoo, MI.

Papa [Papalewis], R. (1988). *Exploring district culture: Administrators' shared values, perceptions, and beliefs of their districts' management model.* Paper presented at the annual conference of the American Educational Research Association, New Orleans, LA. (*Resources in Education ED 298619*).

Papa [Papalewis], R. (1987). *Women and minorities in school administration: What are the barriers of equal access.* Paper presented at the annual conference of the National Council of Professors of Educational Administration, Chadron, NE.

Papa [Papalewis], R. (1987). *Factors and perceptions of equal access for women and minorities in educational administration.* Paper presented at the annual conference of the American Educational Research Association, Washington, DC. (*ERIC Document and Reproduction Service No. ED 283282*).

REFERENCES

Ackerman, R., & Maslin-Ostrowski, P. (2002). *The wounded leader: How real leadership emerges in times of crisis*. San Francisco: Jossey-Bass.

Aldridge, J., & Goldman, R. (2006). *Current issues and trends in education* (2nd ed.). Boston, MA: Allyn & Bacon.

Alexander, K. L., Entwisle, D. R., & Dauber, S. L. (2003). *On the success of failure: A reassessment of the effects of retention in the primary school grades* (2nd ed.). Cambridge, UK: Cambridge University Press.

Allen, R. (2009). Has the time come for national standards? *Association for Supervision and Curriculum Development Info Brief, 15*(2), 1–9.

Ammer, C. (2012, Summer). It's a Zoo: World War II Military Slang. *The Quarterly Journal of Military History, 24*(4), 16–17.

Arizona Department of Education. (2011). *A–F Accountability*. Retrieved June 30, 2012, from www.azed.gov/research-evaluation/a-f-accountability.

Arizona School Facilities Board. (2011). *District Capital Plans*. Retrieved June 30, 2012, from www.azsfb.gov/sfb/sfbscr/sfbda/daChooseTarget.asp.

Aztalk. (2011, April 10). Arizona indicators snapshot: Low household education may hinder children's academic success. *Arizona Republic*, B11.

Baker, C. (2012, June 30). Superintendent. (F. Davidson, Interviewer).

Bandura, A. (2001). Social cognitive theory: An agentic perspective. *Annual review of psychology, 52*, 1–26.

Barber, J. (1985). *The presidential character: Predicting performance in the White House*. Englewood Cliffs, NJ: Prentice Hall.

Barlosky, M. (2006). Knowledge, practical. In F. English (Ed.), *Encyclopedia of educational leadership and administration* (pp. 542–44). Thousand Oaks, CA: Sage.

Barnhart, R. (1995). *The Barnhart concise dictionary of etymology*. New York: HarperCollins.

Barry, B. (2005). *Why social justice matters*. Cambridge, UK: Polity Press.

Barton, P. (2010). National education standards: To be or not to be? *Educational Leadership, 67*(7), 22–29.

Battersby, J. D. (2009). *Nelson Mandela: A life in photographs*. New York: Sterling.

Bauman, Z. (2004). *Identity*. Cambridge, UK: Polity Press.

Becker, G. (1976). *The economic approach to human behavior*. Chicago, IL: University of Chicago Press.

Bennis, W. (1989). *On becoming a leader*. Cambridge, MA: Perseus Books.

Black, S. (2008). *Second time around*. Retrieved from http://www.susanohanian.org/show_research.php?id=63.

Blasé, J., & Blasé, J. (2003). *Breaking the silence: Overcoming the problem of principal mistreatment of teachers*. Thousand Oaks, CA: Corwin Press.

Blount, J. (1998). *Destined to rule the schools: Women and the superintendency in the twentieth century*. Albany, NY: SUNY Press.

Bohman, J. (1992). The limits of rational choice explanation. In J. Coleman and T. Fararo (Eds.), *Rational choice theory: Advocacy and critique* (pp. 207–28). Newbury Park, CA: Sage.

Bolman, L. G., & Deal, E. T. (2001). *Leading with soul*. San Francisco: Jossey-Bass.

Bottery, M. (2004). *The challenge of educational leadership: Values in a globalized age*. London: Paul Chapman.

Bourdieu, P., & Passeron, J.-C. (2000). *Reproduction in education, society and culture* (2nd ed.). London: Sage.

Bourdieu, P. (1999). Understanding. In P. Bourdieu, *The weight of the world: Social suffering in contemporary society* (pp. 607–29). Stanford, CA: Stanford University Press.

Bourdieu, P. (1984). *Distinction: A social critique of the judgment of taste*. R. Nice, Trans. Cambridge, MA: Harvard University Press.

Brady, R. C. (2003). *Can failing schools be fixed?* Washington, DC: Thomas B. Fordham Foundation.

Bredeson, P. V. (1996). Superintendents' roles in curriculum development and instructional leadership: Instructional visionaries, collaborators, supporters, and delegators. *Journal of School Leadership, 6*(3), 243–64.

Britz, D. (2011, April 10). Education: Charter schools try different education models. *Arizona Republic*, B4.

Brookings Institution. (1983). *A Nation at Risk*. Washington, DC.

Brown, R., & Papa, R. (2008, February). *What they don't teach you at the summer leadership institutes*. Presentation at the American Association of State Colleges and Universities winter meeting, Tempe, AZ.

Brown v. Board of Education. (n.d.). Retrieved July 23, 2012, from http://www.nationalcenter.org/brown.html.

Brunner, C. C. (1999). Power, gender, and superintendent selection. In C. C. Brunner (Ed.), *Sacred dreams: Women and the superintendency* (pp. 63–78). Albany, NY: SUNY Press.

Brussell, E. E. (1988). *Webster's new world dictionary of quotable definitions*. Englewood Cliffs, NJ: Prentice Hall.

Buchanan, J. (2004). Personal communication, March 26, 2004.

California Department of Education. (2001). *Academic performance index, api.* Sacramento, CA: California Department of Education, California Department of Education Policy and Evaluation Division.

Cassidy, J. (2009). *How markets fail: The logic of economic calamities.* New York, NY: Farrar, Straus and Giroux.

Chappell, K. (2006, January). Remembering Rosa Parks. *Ebony, 61*(3), 126–32.

Clift, R., Houston, W., & Pugach, M. (Eds.). (1990). *Encouraging reflective practice in education.* New York, NY: Teachers College Press.

Collaborate. (2012). In merriam-webster.com. Retrieved July 22, 2012, from http://www.merriam-webster.com/dictionary/collaborate.

Collins, J. (2001). *Good to great: Why some companies make the leap . . . and others don't.* New York: HarperCollins.

Common Core State Standards Initiative. (2011). *About the standards.* Retrieved May 21, 2012, from http://www.corestandards.org/about-the-standards.

Common Core State Standards Initiative. (2011). *English language arts standards.* Retrieved May 21, 2012, from http://www.corestandards.org/the-standards/english-language-arts-standards/introduction/key-design-considerations/.

Common Core State Standards. (2010). Retrieved July 23, 2012, from www.corestandards.org/.

Common Core State Standards Initiative. (2011). *Mathematics.* Retrieved May 21, 2012, from http://www.corestandards.org/the-standards/mathematics/introduction/standards-for-mathematical-practice/.

Conley, D. (2011). Building on the common core. *Educational Leadership, 68*(6), 16–20.

Covey, S. (1991). *The seven habits of highly successful people.* New York: Simon & Schuster.

Crane Schools. (2011). *Crane Schools fast facts.* Retrieved June 29, 2012, from www.craneschools.org/districtinfo.

Cuban, L. (2001). *Leadership for student learning: Urban school leadership—different in kind and degree.* Washington, DC: Institute for Education Leadership.

Cuban, L. (1984). Transforming the frog into a prince: Effective schools research, policy, and practice at the district level. *Harvard Educational Review, 54*(2), 129–51.

Culver, M. K. (2009). *Applying servant leadership in today's schools.* Larchmont, NY: Eye on Education.

Darrow, R. (2010, April). The bottom line: Funding online courses. *The School Administrator, 67*(4), 26–30.

Davidson, F. (2005). *Superintendent and principal perceptions of superintendent instructional leadership practices in improving school districts.* Tucson: Unpublished doctoral dissertation, University of Arizona.

Deer, C. (2008). Reflexivity. In M. Grenfell, *Pierre Bourdieu: Key concepts.* Durham, UK: Acumen.

DePree, M. (1989). *Leadership is an art.* New York: Bantam Doubleday.

Dessoff, A. (2009). Reaching graduation with credit recovery. *District Administration, 45,* 43–48.

Dewey, J. (1938). *Experience and education.* New York: Collier Books.

Eckblad, M. (2010, August 11). Wells Fargo must pay in overdraft-fee case. *The Wall Street Journal*, C13.

Ehrich, L. C., & English, F. (2012). Leadership as dance: A consideration of the applicability of the "mother" of all arts as the basis for establishing connoisseurship. *International Journal of Leadership in Education: Theory and Practice, 15*(4).

Eide, E. R., & Showalter, M. H. (2001). The effect of grade retention on education and labor market outcomes. *Economics of Education Review, 20,* 563.

Eisner, E. W. (2005). *Reimagining schools: The selected works of Elliot W. Eisner.* New York, NY: Routledge.

EKR. (2011, October 2). Educated guesswork: How does the kobayashi maru test make any sense? Retrieved July 22, 2012, from http://www.educatedguesswork.org/2011/10/how_does_the_kobayashi_maru_te.html.

English, F., Papa, R., Mullen, C., & Creighton, T. (2012). *Educational leadership at 2050: Conjectures, challenges, and promises.* Lanham, MD: Rowman & Littlefield.

English, F., Papa, R., Mullen, C., Creighton, T., & Berry, J. (2011, November). *Reverse casting educational leadership at the mid-century: Evocations of time travel.* A presentation—fireside chats at the annual conference of the University Council of Educational Administration, Pittsburgh, PA.

English, F. (2011). Educational leadership at century's beginning—A continuing search for the philosopher's stone. In F. English (Ed.), *The Sage handbook of educational leadership, 2nd ed.* (pp. vii–xiii). Thousand Oaks, CA: Sage.

English, F., Papa, R., & Mullen, C. (2011, August). *Blazing new trails: Preparing leaders for improving access and equity in tomorrow's schools.* National Council of Professors of Educational Administration Annual Conference, Portland, OR.

English, F. (2010). *Deciding what to teach and test: Developing, aligning, and leading the curriculum* (3rd ed.). Thousand Oaks, CA: Corwin.

English, F. (2008). *The art of educational leadership: Balancing performance and accountability.* Thousand Oaks, CA: Sage.

English, F., & Bolton, C. (2008, January). An exploration of administrative heuristics in the United States and the United Kingdom. *Journal of School Leadership, 18*(1), 96–119.

English, F. (2007). The NRC's scientific research in education: It isn't even wrong. In F. English and G. C. Furman (Eds.), *Research and educational leadership: Navigating the new National Research Council Guidelines* (pp. 1–38). Lanham, MD: Rowman & Littlefield Education.

English, F. (2002, January). The penetration of educational leadership texts by revelation and prophecy: The case of Stephen R. Covey. *Journal of School Leadership, 12*(7), 4–22.

Faller, M. B. (2012, March 9). Number of kids eligible for lunch subsidy stable: Figures from Northeast Valley schools reflect fall 2010. *Arizona Republic,* B2.

Fischer, L. (1950). *The life of Mahatma Gandhi.* New York, NY: Harper & Brothers.

Foucault, M. (1980). *Power/knowledge.* C. Gordon (Ed.). New York, NY: Pantheon Books.

Foucault, M. (1974). *The archaeology of knowledge.* London: Tavistock.

Freund, W., & Andrews, E. A. (1854). *A copious and critical Latin-English lexicon.* New York: Harper & Brothers.

Frey, N. (2005). Retention, social promotion, and academic redshirting: What do we know and need to know? *Remedial & Special Education, 26,* 332–46. doi:http://www.ingenta connect.com/content/proedcw/rase.

Fryand, D. J., & Capper, C. A. (2003). Do you have any idea who you just hired? A study of open and closeted sexual minority K–12 administrators. *Journal of School Leadership, 13*(1), 86–124.

Fullan, M. (2008). *The six secrets of change.* San Francisco: Jossey-Bass.

Gardner, H. (1995). *Leading minds: An anatomy of leadership.* New York: HarperCollins.

Gardner, J. W. (1968). *No easy victories.* H. Rowan (Ed.). New York: Harper Colophon Books.

Gilbert, M. (1991). *Churchill: A life.* New York, NY: Henry Holt and Company.

Gill, B. (1987). *Many masks: A life of Frank Lloyd Wright.* New York: DeCapo Press.

Glendale Union High School District. (2004–2012). *Legacy of learning: Yesterday, today and tomorrow.* Retrieved June 30, 2012, from www.guhsdaz.org.

Gordon, E. W., & Bridglall, B. L. (2005). The challenge, context, and the preconditions of academic development at high levels. In E. W. Gordon, B. L. Bridgalall, and A. S. Meroe (Eds.), *Supplementary education: The hidden curriculum of high academic achievement* (pp. 59–79). Lanham, MD: Rowman & Littlefield,

Greenleaf, R. K. (1970). *The servant as leader.* Indianapolis, IN: The Robert Greenleaf Center.

Grenfell, M. (2007). *Pierre Bourdieu: Education and training.* London, UK: P Continuum.

Hall, E. T. (1959). *The silent language.* Greenwich, CT: Fawcett Premier Books.

Hallinger, P., & Heck, R. H. (2011). Collaborative leadership and school improvement: Understanding the impact on school capacity and student learning. In T. Townsend & J. MacBeath (Eds.), *International handbook of leadership for learning* (chapter 27, pp. 469–85). Dordrecht, Holland: Springer.

Hansen, R. J. (2011, April 7). Ariz. kids becoming more diverse: State's youths less like state's adults in ethnicity than elsewhere in U.S. *Arizona Republic,* B6.

Hecht, J. M. (2003). *Doubt: A history.* San Francisco, CA: HarperCollins.

Heilbrunn, J. (1996). Can leadership be studied? In P. Temes (Ed.), *Teaching leadership: Essays in theory and practice* (pp. 1–12). New York, NY: Peter Lang.

Heywood, J. (2005). A comment on identity, the curriculum, and educational policy. In L. E. Watson & J. Heywood (Eds.), *Identity and inclusion in education: Some Irish and other European perspectives* (pp. 43–58). European Forum on Educational Administration. Sheffield, UK: Hallam University.

Hoffer, E. (1955). *The passionate state of mind.* New York, NY: Harper & Row.

Holland, D., & Lave, J. (2001). History in person, an introduction. In D. Holland & J. Lave (Eds.), *History in person.* Santa Fe, NM: School of American Research Press.

Hoy, W. K. (2003). An analysis of enabling and mindful school structures. *Journal of Educational Administration, 41*(1), 87–108.

HR 6244. (2010). *Race to the top act.* Retrieved from www.opencongress.org/bill/111-h6244/show.

Hu, W. (2008, June 25). Holding back young students: Is program a gift or a stigma? *The New York Times.* Retrieved from http://www.nytimes.com/2008/06/25/.

Johnson, J. (2012, June 25). Superintendent. (F. Davidson, Interviewer).

Johnson, S. (2002). *Who moved my cheese?* New York: G. P. Putnam & Sons.

Karweit, N. (1991, May). *Repeating a grade: Time to grow or denial of opportunity?* Center for Research and Improvement (Report No. 16). Retrieved from http://www.eric.ed.gov/PDFS/ED336493.pdf.

Keegan, J. (2002). *Winston Churchill.* New York: Penguin Books.

Keegan, J. (1987). *The mask of command.* New York, NY: Viking.

Khurana, R. (2002). *Searching for a corporate savior: The irrational quest for charismatic CEOs.* Princeton, NJ: Princeton University Press.

Koebler, P. (2011, October). ABOR panel, comments made by Paul Koebler from WestEd. At the Annual Superintendents and Higher Education Division Conference, Prescott, AZ.

Koschoreck, J. W. (2001). Accountability and educational equity in the transformation of an urban school district. *Education and Urban Society, 33*(3), 284–304.

Kowalski, T. (1995). *Keepers of the flame: Contemporary urban superintendents.* Thousand Oaks: Corwin Press, Inc.

LeFanu, J. (1999). *The rise and fall of modern medicine.* New York, NY: Carroll & Graf.

Leithwood, K., & Sun, J. (2012, August). The nature and effects of transformational school leadership: A meta-analytic review of unpublished research. *Educational Administration Quarterly, 48*(3), 387–423.

Leithwood, K., Louis, K. S., Anderson, S., & Wahlstrom, K. (2004). *Review of research: How leadership influences student learning.* New York: The Wallace Foundation.

Leithwood, K., & Earl, L. (2000). Education accountability effects: An international perspective. *Peabody Journal of Education, 74*(4), 1–18.

Lewis, A. C. (2003). From universal access to universal proficiency. *The School Administrator, 60*(8), 14–16, 18–20.

Loeffler, C., Creighton, T., & Papa, R. (2005). *Virtual success: The relationship of adult learning styles and success in online graduate education leadership programs.* Presentation at the annual conference of the National Council of Professors of Educational Administration Summit on the Preparation of School Leaders, Washington, DC.

Lopez, G. (2003). The (racially neutral) politics of education: A critical race theory perspective. *Educational Administration Quarterly, 39*(1) 68–94.

Loughran, J. (1996). *Developing reflective practice: Learning about teaching and learning through modeling.* London, UK: Falmer Press.

Lumby, J., & English, F. (2009, June). From simplicism to complexity in leadership identity and preparation: Exploring the lineage and dark secrets. *International Journal of Leadership in Education, 12*(2), 95–114.

Maalouf, A. (2000). *Identity.* London: Harvil.

McCullough, D. (1992). *Truman.* New York, NY: Simon & Schuster.

Meier, D., Schmidt, W., Finn, C., Schlechty, P., & Zhao, Y. (2010). Are national standards the right move? *Educational Leadership, 67*(7), 30–36.

Morgan, E. S. (2002). *Benjamin Franklin.* New Haven, CT: Yale University Press.

Morrill, R. L. (2007). *Strategic leadership: Integrating strategy and leadership in colleges and universities.* Lanham, MD: Rowman & Littlefield.

Mullen, C. (2012). Mentoring: An overview. In S. J. Fletcher & C. A. Mullen (Eds.), *The SAGE Handbook of Mentoring and Coaching in Education* (pp. 7–23). Thousand Oaks, CA: Sage.

Murphy, J. (2002). Reculturing the profession of educational leadership: New blueprints. *Educational Administration Quarterly, 38*(2), 176–91.

Murphy, J. (2000, October–December). A response to English. *International Journal of Leadership in Education, 3*(4), 399–410.

Murphy, J., & Hallinger, P. (1988). Characteristics of instructionally effective school districts. *Journal of Educational Research, 81*(3), 175–81.

Murphy, J., & Hallinger, P. (1986). The superintendent as instructional leader: Findings from effective school districts. *Journal of Educational Administration, 24*(3), 213–36.

NASA. (2007). *Sputnik and dawn of the space age.* Retrieved July 23, 2012, from http:// history.nasa.gov/sputnik/.

National Governors Association Center for Best Practices, Council of Chief State School Officers. (2010). *Common core state standards.* Washington, DC.: National Governors Association Center for Best Practices and Council of Chief State School Officers.

National Research Council (NRC) Committee on Scientific Principles for Education Research (2002). In R. J. Shavelson & L. Towne (Eds.), *Scientific research in education.* Washington, DC: National Academy Press.

NCLB. (2001). No Child Left Behind. Retrieved July 23, 2012, from http://www.ed.gov/esea.

NEPC-National Educational Policy Center. (n.d.). Retrieved July 24, 2012, from http:// nepc.colorado.edu/think-tank-reviews.

Nestor-Baker, N., & Hoy, W. (2001, February). Tacit knowledge of school superintendents: Its nature, meaning, and content. *Educational Administration Quarterly, 37*(1), 86–129.

Nielsen, J. S. (2004). *The myth of leadership: Creating leaderless organizations.* Palo Alto, CA: Davies-Black Publishing.

Nuland, S. B. (2003). *The doctors' plague: Germs, childbirth fever, and the strange story of Ignac Semmelweis.* New York, NY: Norton.

Nussbaum, D. (2007, September 9). Calling all superintendents. *New York Times,* section 14NJ, p. 1.

Obama, B. (2009, March 10). *Remarks by the President to the Hispanic Chamber of Commerce on a complete and competitive American education.* Retrieved May 21, 2012, from www.whitehouse.gov/the_press_office/Remarks-of-the-President-to-the-United-States -Hispanic-Chamber-of-Commerce.

Osterman, K., & Kottkamp, R. (1993). *Reflective practice for educators: Improving schooling through professional development.* Newbury Park, CA: Corwin Press.

Palestini, R. (2012). *A commonsense approach to educational leadership: Lessons from the founders.* Lanham, MD: Rowman & Littlefield.

Papa, R., Kain, D., & Brown, R. (in press). *Who moved my theory? A kitsch exploration of kitsch leadership texts.* In G. Brown & B. Irby (Eds.), *Handbook of educational theories.* Charlotte, NC: Information Age Publishing.

Papa, R. (2012). Activist leadership: Walter D. Cocking lecture 2011. In G. Perreault and L. Zellner (Eds.), *Yearbook 2012 social justice, competition and quality: 21st century leadership challenges,* National Council of Professors of Educational Administration.

Papa, R. (2011). Standards for educational leadership: Promises, paradoxes and pitfalls. In F. English (Ed.), *Handbook of educational leadership, 2nd ed.* (pp. 195–209). Thousand Oaks, CA: Sage.

Papa, R., & English, F. (2011). *Turn around principals for under-performing schools.* Lanham, MD: Rowman & Littlefield.

Papa, R., & Papa, J. (2011). Leading adult learners: Preparing future leaders and professional development of those they lead. In R. Papa (Ed.), *Technology leadership for school improvement.* Thousand Oaks, CA: Sage.

Papa, R., & Brown, R. (2011, November). *English language policy in Arizona schools: Blind to its own blindness.* Poster presentation at the Language, Education and Diversity Conference, University of Auckland, New Zealand.

Papa, R., Culver, M., & Schwanenberger, M. (2011, August). *12 year empirical study on school leader best practices.* National Council of Professors of Educational Administration Annual Conference, Portland, OR.

Papa, R. (2011, August). High achieving Arizona public schools. *Arizona School Administrators Update.* Phoenix, AZ: Arizona School Administrators Publications.

Papa, R. (2011, May). The accoutrements of leadership. *Arizona School Administrators Update.* Phoenix, AZ: Arizona School Administrators Publications.

Papa, R., Culver, M., & Schwanenberger, M. (2011, April). *Leadership characteristics to turn around underperforming schools: Empirical research update.* Arizona Professors of Educational Administration, Annual Conference, Phoenix, AZ.

Papa, R., & Brown, R. (2011, January). *Leadership characteristics to turn around underperforming schools.* International Conference on Education, Honolulu, HI.

Papa, R. (Panel organizer). (2007, November). *Updating the national standards for school leaders.* University Council of Educational Administration, Annual conference, Washington, DC.

Papa, R., Loeffler, C., & Creighton, T. (2006). The relationship of adult learning styles and success in online graduate education. Presentation at the annual conference of the American Educational Research Association, San Francisco.

Papa [Papalewis], R., & Fortune, R. (2003). *Promising site leadership practices for schools with African-American and Latino students.* At the annual conference of the National School Boards Association, San Francisco.

Papa [Papalewis], R., & Fortune, R. (2002). *Leadership on purpose: Promising practices for African American and Hispanic students.* Thousand Oaks, CA: Corwin Publications.

Papa [Papalewis], R. (2002). *Promising leadership practices for principals.* Paper presented at the annual conference of the National Council of Professors of Educational Administration, Burlington, VT.

Papa [Papalewis], R., & Lee, E. (2002). *Promising site leadership practices for African-American and Latino students.* At the annual conference of American Educational Research Association, New Orleans, LA.

Papa [Papalewis], R., & Kramer, G. L. (2002). *Mentoring, advising, and supporting students.* National Conference on Higher Education Communities of Practice, American Educational Research Association, Chicago, IL.

Papa [Papalewis], R., & Brown, R. (1998). *Leadership required for the new millennium.* Paper presented at the annual conference of the National Council of Professors of Educational Administration, Juneau, AK.

Papa [Papalewis], R. (1998). *Promising practices in educational administration programs.* Discussant for SIG/Teaching in Educational Administration at the annual conference of the American Educational Research Association Conference, San Diego, CA.

Papa [Papalewis], R. (1991). *Preparing school administrators for the culturally and linguistically diverse: A formal mentor training program in progress.* Paper presented at the annual conference of the American Educators Research Association, Chicago, IL. *(Resources in Education ED 333 094).*

Papa [Papalewis], R. (1990). *What we are becoming we are: Educational administration for the 21st century.* Paper presented at the annual conference of the National Council of Professors of Educational Administration, Los Angeles, CA. *(Resources in Education ED 328 166).*

Papa [Papalewis], R. (1989). *A national challenge: The underrepresented in education.* Paper presented at the annual conference of the National Council of Professors of Educational Administration, Birmingham, AL.

Papa [Papalewis], R., & Brown, R. (1989). *Gender communication style and student evaluation of instruction.* Colloquium, University of Sydney, Australia.

Papa [Papalewis], R. (1989). *Gender characteristics of teaching and evaluation measures of instruction.* Presentation at the annual conference of the American Educational Research Association, San Francisco, CA.

Papa [Papalewis], R. (1988). *Artistry through symbolic language.* Paper presented at the annual conference of the National Council of Professors of Educational Administration, Kalamazoo, MI.

Papa [Papalewis], R. (1988). *Exploring district culture: Administrators' shared values, perceptions, and beliefs of their districts' management model.* Paper presented at the annual conference of the American Educational Research Association, New Orleans, LA. *(Resources in Education No. ED 298619).*

Papa [Papalewis], R. (1987). *Women and minorities in school administration: What are the barriers of equal access.* Paper presented at the annual conference of the National Council of Professors of Educational Administration, Chadron, NE.

Papa [Papalewis], R. (1987). *Factors and perceptions of equal access for women and minorities in educational administration.* Paper presented at the annual conference of the American Educational Research Association, Washington, DC. *(ERIC Document and Reproduction Service No. ED 283282).*

Papa [Papalewis], R. (1987). The relationship of selected variables to mentoring in doctoral level education. *International Journal of Mentoring, 1*(1), 22–26.

Peirce, C. S. (1955). *Philosophical writings of Peirce.* J. Buchler (Ed.). New York, NY: Dover.

Peters, C. (2005). *Five days in Philadelphia.* New York: Public Affairs.

Petersen, G. (1999). Demonstrated actions of instructional leaders: An examination of five California superintendents. *Education Policy Analysis Archives, 7*(18).

Petersen, P. E. (1983). *Making the grade.* Retrieved July 23, 2012, from http://www.eric .ed.gov/ERICWebPortal/search/detailmini.jsp?_nfpb=true&_&ERICExtSearch_Search Value_0=ED233112&ERICExtSearch_SearchType_0=no&accno=ED233112.

Peterson, K. D., & Cosner, S. (2006). Culture, school. In F. English (Ed.), *Encyclopedia of educational leadership and administration, Vol. 1.* (pp. 249–51). Thousand Oaks, CA: Sage,

Pfeffer, J. (2007). *What were they thinking?: Unconventional wisdom about management.* Boston: Harvard Business School Press.

Polanyi, M. (1967). *The tacit dimension.* New York, NY: Anchor Books.

Potter, A., & Emerson, G. B. (1842). *The school and the schoolmaster.* New York: Harper & Brothers.

Quinn, D. M. (2002). The impact of principal leadership behaviors on instructional practice and student engagement. *Journal of Educational Administration, 40*(5), 427–47.

Rhode, M., & Shaffer, D. W. (2004). Us, ourselves, and we: Thoughts about social (self-) categorization. *Association for Computing Machinery (ACM), SigGROUP Bulletin 24* (3), 19–24.

Rost, J. C. (1991). *Leadership for the twenty-first century.* New York: Praeger.

Rothman, R. (2012). A common core of readiness. *Educational Leadership, 69*(7), 11–15.

Sackville-West, V. (1936). *Saint Joan of Arc.* New York: The Literary Guild.

Sagan, C. (n.d.). Quote. Retrieved July 23, 2012, from http://www.thinkexist.com/English/ Author/x/Author_2479_1.htm.

Scheurich, J. J., & Skrla, L. (2003). *Leadership for equity and excellence: Creating high-achievement classrooms, schools, and districts.* Thousand Oaks, CA: Sage.

Schiff, K. (2005). *Lighting the way: Nine women who changed modern America.* New York, NY: Hyperion.

Schon, D. (1987). *Educating the reflective practitioner. Toward a new design for teaching and learning in the professions.* San Francisco, CA: Jossey-Bass.

Schon, D. (1983). *The reflective practitioner: How professionals think in action.* New York, NY: Basic Books.

Schweitzer, A. (1965). *The teaching of reverence for life.* Richard and Clara Winston, Trans. New York: Holt, Rinehart and Winston.

Scott-Kilvert, I. (1960). *Plutarch: The rise and fall of Athens.* London, England: The Folio Society.

Shaffer, D. W. (2009). Epistemic network analysis: A prototype for 21st century assessment of learning. *International Journal of Learning and Media, 1*(2), 1–21.

Shakeshaft, C. (2011). Wild patience: Women in school administration. In F. English (Ed.), *The Sage handbook of educational leadership, 2nd ed.* (pp. 210–23). Thousand Oaks, CA: Sage.

Silberglitt, B., Appleton, J., Burns, M., & Jimerson, S. (2006). Examining the effects of grade retention on student reading performance: A longitudinal study. *Journal of School Psychology, 44*, 255–70.

Simon, R., & McGrane, V. (2011, July 21). Wells penalty: $85 million. *The Wall Street Journal*, C3.

Spartacus Educational. (n.d.). *Domino theory.* Retrieved July 22, 2012, from http://www .spartacus.schoolnet.co.uk/COLDdomino.htm.

Stoll, L., & Fink, D. (1996). The power of school culture. In *Changing our schools* (pp. 80–100). Buckingham, UK: Open University Press.

Stratton, W. K. (2012, July 7–8). Hamlet in the ring. *The Wall Street Journal*, C5.

Tallerico, M. (2012). *Leading curriculum improvement: Fundamentals for school principals*. Lanham, MD: Rowman & Littlefield.

The Economist (2004, August 21). How 51 gorillas can make you seriously rich, 69.

The Quotations Page. (n.d.). *Sir Francis Bacon*. Retrieved on June 9, 2012, from http://www.quotationspage.com/search.php3.

The Quotations Page. (n.d.). *Thales*. Retrieved on June 9, 2012, from http://www.quotationspage.com/search/php3.

The Wall Street Journal. (2010, October 21). Angelo's ashes, A16.

Thompson, C., & Cunningham, E. (2000, December). Retention and social promotion: Research and implications for policy. *The Educational Resources Information Center (ERIC)*, Digest Number 161: ERIC identifier ED449241.

Timiraos, N., & Bray, C. (2011, December 17–18). SEC brings crisis-era suits. *The Wall Street Journal*, B1.

Togneri, W. (2003). *Beyond islands of excellence: What districts can do to improve instruction and achievement in all schools*. Washington, DC: Learning First Alliance.

Tuchman, B. (1979). *A distant mirror*. New York: Alfred A. Knopf.

Twentieth Century Task Force on Federal Educational Policy. (1983). Making the Grade. New York: Priority Pr Pubns.

Tyack, D. (1974). *The one best system: A history of urban education*. Cambridge, MA: Harvard University Press.

Umpstead, B. (2009). The rise of online learning. *Principal Leadership*, 1, 68–70.

Vail Unified School District. (2012). *Where education is a community effort*. Retrieved June 30, 2012, from www.vail.k12.az.us.

Van Manen, V. (1977). Linking ways of knowing with ways of being practical. *Curriculum Inquiry, 6* (3), 205–28.

Wagner, L. K. (2010). *The savvy superintendent: Leading instruction to the top of the class*. Lanham, MD: Rowman & Littlefield.

Wagner, T. (2001). Leadership for learning: An action theory of school change. *Phi Delta Kappan, 82*(5), 378–83.

Watkins, M. D. (2012, June). How managers become leaders. *Harvard Business Review*, 90(6), 65–72.

Webb, J., Schirato, T., & Danaher, G. (2002). *Understanding Bourdieu*. London: Sage.

Wheeler, J. J. (2012). *North Carolina superintendent turnover*. Unpublished doctoral dissertation, University of North Carolina at Chapel Hill.

Wit and Wisdom. (2012, July 6–11). *The Week*, p. 17.

Xia, C., & Glennie, E. (2005, January). *Grade retention: A flawed education strategy*. Durham, NC: Center for Child and Family Policy, Duke University.

York-Barr, J., Sommers, W., Ghere, G., & Montie, J. (2001). *Reflective practice to improve schools: An action guide for educators*. Thousand Oaks, CA: Corwin Press.

INDEX

accoutering, xii, 68

accoutrements, 9, 73, 77, 79, 89, 91, 106

Acheson, D., 33

Ackerman, R., 73

adult learners, 9, 90

agency, human, 10

Arizona, 86–87

Bacon, F., 38

Barber, J., 71

Barry, B., 46

behavioral/structural/functional focus (BSF), xi

Bennis, W., 52, 70

best practices, 86

Blount, J., 36

Bolton, C., 15

Bottery, M., 73

Bourdieu, P., 12, 46, 75

Brown, R., 38

Brown v. Board of Education, 50

Brunner, C., 36

Casa Grande Elementary School District, Arizona, 101

character, 72

charisma, xii

charismatic CEOs, 6

Churchill, W., 9, 34, 77

cohesion, 2

Collins, J., 7

commanders, battlefield, 7

common core standards, 40–46

community of practice, 4

context, 7, 74

contextual leadership, 21

Council of Chief State School Officers, 51

Crane Elementary School District, Arizona, 102

Creighton, T., 9, 74, 93

Cuban, L., 56

cultural arbitrary, 45

culture, 74

curriculum, 40; common, 54; unintended, 40

Davidson, F., 53

Dewey, J., 12

digital learning environment, 4

direct effects model, 11

discourse, 36
dogma, 35–36

efficient market hypothesis, 17
Ehrich, L., 74, 112
Eisner, E., 91
English, F., 9, 15, 37, 68, 93
epistemic orientation, 5
epistemology, 4

failing schools, 20
Fannie Mae, 8
followers, 98
Fortune, R., 9, 28, 54, 83
Foucault, M., 35, 39
Franklin, B., 77
Freddie Mac, 8
Fullan, M., 49, 52, 56

Galen, 36
Gandhi, M., 34
Gardner, J., 70, 79
Glendale Union High School District,
    Arizona, 103
great leadership, 5
Greenleaf, R., 20

habits of reflection, 19
Hallinger, P., 10–11, 58
Heck, R., 10–11
herd behavior, 17
heroic figures, 6
heroic leadership, 5, 11
Heywood, J., 6
high stakes testing, 50
Hispanic Chamber of Commerce, 44
Hoffer, E., 1
Huerta, Dolores, 34

identity, 5–6, 72; as continua, 7; fluid nature
    of, 6

imaginativeness, 10
instruction, 22
ISLLC/ELCC standards, xiii

Jeanne d'Arc, 68

Kain, D., 38
Keegan, J., 7, 77
kitsch management, 38
knowledge, 5; in action, 13; as dogma, 37;
    as power, 38; research based, 37; of self,
    33, 97
Kowalski, T., 53

language, common, 55
leaderless organizations, 3
leadership, 67; as accoutrement, 6;
    collaborative, 11, 29; distributed, 96;
    generic, 38; greatness, 81; heroic, 96;
    instructional, 24; servant, 20;
    time, 61
leadership for school improvement,
    10–11
learning communities, 30
Leithwood, K., 79
Lumby, J., 5, 74

Making the Grade, 50
management time, 61
managerial trap, 97
Mandela, N., 70
Maslin-Ostrowski, P., 73
mentoring, 39
misrecognition, 46
Mozilo, A., 8
Mullen, C., 9, 40, 74, 93, 115
Murphy, J., 53, 58, 115

National Education Policy Center, 37
National Governors Association, 51
National Research Council, 37

A Nation at Risk, 50
Nehru, J., 2
No Child Left Behind Act, 41

Obama, B., 44
optimism, 27

Papa, R., 9, 20, 28, 38, 39, 54, 68, 83, 90
parent-child relationship, 99
Parks, R., 69
Pasteur, L., 36
Patterson, F., 70
philosopher's stone, 35
Pierce, C., 35
Plutarch, 34
politics, 19
power, 32
principal, 54

racism, 36–37
rational choice theory, 15–16
reflect, 74
reflection, 13
reflective evaluation craft, 13
reflective practice, xiii, 13
reflective thinking, 13
reflexive practice, xiii, 13–14
retention, 41
Roosevelt, F., 67, 77
Rost, J., 67

Sagan, C., 83
Schon, D., 14, 118
school choice, 50
school culture, 11–12

Schweitzer, A., 81
sexism, 36
Shakeshaft, C., 38
Shakespeare, 34, 38
skills, 5
social cognitive theory, 63
Sputnik, 49
students, 21
style, 72
superintendent, 29, 53, 76

tacit knowledge, 13
teacher induction programs, 26
teachers, 25
teamwork, 29
technology, 43
Thales, 34
Truman, H., 33–34
trust, 29
Tuchman, B., 68
turnaround efforts for schools, 20
Tutu, D., 71

ubuntu, 70

Vail Unified School District, Arizona, 103
values, 19; habitual, 30

War on Poverty, 50
wealth distribution, 46
Wells Fargo, 8
Wheeler, J., 70, 73, 76
wisdom of the field, 36
world view, 71
Wright, F., 72

ABOUT THE AUTHORS

Dr. Rosemary Papa currently serves as The Del and Jewel Lewis Endowed Chair in Learning Centered Leadership and Professor of Educational Leadership in the College of Education at Northern Arizona University—a position she has held since 2007. Her record of publications includes twelve books as author or coauthor, numerous book chapters, monographs, and over eighty referred journal articles. She has served as a principal and chief school administrator for two districts in Nebraska; California State University system level assistant vice chancellor for academic affairs; vice president for Sylvan Learning, Inc.; faculty director of a university-based center for teaching and learning in California; and founded two joint doctoral programs in educational leadership with University of California universities. She has worked internationally as a noted educator with expertise in leadership characteristics known as *accoutrements*, mentoring, adult learning, and multimedia technology. She may be contacted at Rosemary.Papa@nau.edu.

Dr. Fenwick English currently is the R. Wendell Eaves Senior Distinguished Professor of Educational Leadership in the School of Education at the University of North Carolina at Chapel Hill, a position he has held since 2001. Dr. English is the author or coauthor of over thirty-five books and has presented his research over two decades at the American Educational Research Association Divisions A and L; National Council of Professors of Educational Administration; University Council of Educational Administration; British Educational Leadership and Management Society; and the Commonwealth Council for Educational Administration. He and Rosemary Papa have coauthored many texts including *Restoring Human Agency to Educational Administration: Status and Strategies* (2010); *Turnaround Principals for Underperforming Schools* (2011); and *Educational Leadership at 2050: Conjectures, Challenges, and Promises* (2012). He was the president of NCPEA (2011–2012) and of UCEA (2006-2007) respectively. As an educational practitioner, he has held the positions of assistant principal and middle school principal (California); assistant superintendent of schools (Florida); superintendent of schools (New York); associate executive director of the AASA (Virginia); national practice director of elementary and secondary education for Peat, Marwick, Mitchell & Co. (Washington, DC); department chair, University of Cincinnati (Ohio); dean, School of Education at Indiana University-Purdue University in Fort Wayne, and later vice chancellor of academic affairs (Indiana). He is the acknowledged *father* of the curriculum management audit and has worked in many of the large urban school systems in the United States. He may be contacted at fenglish@attglobal.net.

Dr. Frank Davidson began his career in education serving as a Peace Corps volunteer in Paraguay and has been a K–12 teacher and principal, curriculum administrator, and superintendent. He is the past president of the Superintendents' Division of the Arizona School Administrators; in 2000, he received the Arizona School Administrators' All-Arizona Superintendent Award for Large School Districts; and in 2006, he was selected as Arizona Superintendent of the Year and was named as Arizona's nominee for the American Association of School Administrators Superintendent of the Year Award. He is the superintendent of the Casa Grande Elementary School District, a position he has held since 1997. He may be contacted at Frank.Davidson@cgelem.k12.az.us.

Dr. Mary K. Culver is an associate professor of educational leadership at Northern Arizona University. Specializing in curriculum and instructional supervision, she has served as a program manager, director of satellite schools, assistant principal, and principal in the public school system of Arizona. She has published "Applying Servant Leadership in Today's

Schools" and many articles on leadership and serves as consultant to multiple schools in instruction and teacher evaluation. Dr. Culver graduated from Arizona State University with a bachelor of science degree in statistical history, and again with a master of education in curriculum and instruction, with her terminal degree in educational leadership from Northern Arizona University. She may be contacted at Mary.Culver@nau.edu.

Dr. Ric Brown served six years as the chief academic officer (provost/vice president for academic affairs) at California State University, Sacramento, until his retirement in 2007. In addition to being a professor for over thirty years, he held the positions of associate vice president for graduate studies and research at Sacramento and director of university grants and research at California State University, Fresno. His academic areas include statistics, research, measurement, and evaluation. He has published extensively and had a book on higher education administration published in fall 2008. He currently serves as adjunct faculty at Northern Arizona University (teaching statistics and higher education classes) and resides in Sedona, Arizona. He may be contacted at Ric.Brown@nau.edu.